The Confidence to
Write

The Confidence to

Write

A Guide for Overcoming Fear and

Developing Identity as a Writer

Liz Prather | Foreword by Thomas Newkirk

HEINEMANN
Portsmouth, NH

Heinemann

145 Maplewood Avenue, Suite 300

Portsmouth, NH 03801

www.heinemann.com

Heinemann's authors have devoted their entire careers to developing the unique content in their works, and their written expression is protected by copyright law. We respectfully ask that you do not adapt, reuse, or copy anything on third-party (whether for-profit or not-for-profit) lesson-sharing websites.

—**Heinemann Publishers**

The author and publisher wish to thank those who have generously given permission to reprint borrowed material:

Excerpt from *Shoptalk: Learning to Write with Writers*. Copyright © 1990 by Donald M. Murray. Reprinted by permission of The Rosenberg Group on behalf of the Author's estate.

Table adapted from "The Empirical Development of an Instrument to Measure Writing Apprehension" by John A. Daly and Michael D. Miller from *Research in the Teaching of English*, Vol. 9, No. 3 (Winter, 1975). Copyright © 1975 by the National Council of Teachers of English. Reprinted by permission of the author.

Credits continue on page vi.

Library of Congress Cataloging-in-Publication Data

Names: Prather, Liz, author.

Title: The confidence to write : a guide for overcoming fear and developing
   identity as a writer / Liz Prather.

Description: Portsmouth, NH : Heinemann Publishing, [2022] | Includes
   bibliographical references.

Identifiers: LCCN 2021049106 | ISBN 9780325132808

Subjects: LCSH: English language—Composition and exercises—Study and
   teaching (Secondary) | English language—Composition and
   exercises—Study and teaching (Middle school) | English
   language—Composition and exercises—Study and teaching—Psychological
   aspects. | Authorship—Psychological aspects. | Performance anxiety.

Classification: LCC LB1631 .P6747 2022 | DDC
   808/.0420712—dc23/eng/20220110

LC record available at https://lccn.loc.gov/2021049106

Editor: Thomas Newkirk

Production Editor: Sean Moreau

Cover and Interior Designer: Monica Ann Cohen

Typesetter: Shawn Girsberger

Manufacturing: Val Cooper

Printed in the United States of America on acid-free paper.

1 2 3 4 5 VP 26 25 24 23 22   PO 34006

to
Sharon Toadrine
&
Lynda Umfress

Contents

PART ONE

The Case for Discovering Writing Identity & Developing Writing Courage

PART TWO

Discovering Writing Identity

PART THREE

Developing Writing Courage

Acknowledgments

Big thanks to the Heinemann team: Cindy Black, Kim Cahill, Monica Ann Cohen, Michelle Flynn, Sarah Fournier, Suzanne Heiser, Krysten Lebel, Sean Moreau, Katie Ray, Roderick Spelman, Lynette Winegarner; my editor Tom Newkirk; and Catrina Swasey, who, even while working remotely during the pandemic, returned my emails and answered my questions with the speed of light.

So many teacher friends gave me encouragement along the way. Thank you to super teacher Sasha Reinhardt to whom I floated the idea of this book over tacos in May 2019; Lafayette High School's Writing Program leader Holly Ybarrola and the Lafayette Writing Committee; my colleague Venecia Proctor, who shared her students, her joy of teaching, and her great ideas about identity; and my boon companions, Chris McCurry and Amanda Wright, who read the entire manuscript in its final stages and gave me invaluable feedback and insight on structure and tone.

Salute and love to my home team who cheered me through drafts and revisions: Amy Gilliam, Brenda Hatton, Janet Johnson, Stacy Lyons, Kevin Osbourne (who gave me the ending I didn't know I needed), Marge Purdon, Austen Reilley, and Stephanie Smith.

Many, many, many thanks to the students who have shared their stories, their identities, and their lives with me in room 303. Your contribution to my growth as a teacher and as a human has been instrumental to my growth as a writer.

And finally to Paul, my best, last, and forever champion, editor, coconspirator, and sweetheart.

Foreword

As Dorothy and her cohorts close in on the Great Oz, his voice powerfully warns them away—"Do you presume to criticize the Great Oz? . . . The Great Oz has spoken!" But as we all know, Dorothy's dog, Toto, pulls a curtain to reveal that Oz is just a short, plump, timid man whose voice is amplified by a microphone—in his own words, once revealed, a "humbug."

This scene has always been for me a metaphor for writing. Any printed text looks so authoritative, so Oz-like. One word follows the next in beautiful order, unhesitatingly, in this case in Sabon Roman type. Paragraph after paragraph, no pauses, no scratch outs, no images like those below to indicate either a pause for caffeine or indecisiveness or confusion.

This text—any text really—is an act of deception, or at least a performance with all the backstage, rehearsals, and false starts hidden from view, not to mention the doubts, anxieties, and insecurities of the writers themselves, who are, after all, only fallible humans.

In *The Confidence to Write*, Liz Prather pulls back the curtain on writing, and, with surgical precision, takes on the myths, doubts, inhibitions, and avoidances that get in our (and our students') way.

The central barrier has to do not with skills, but identity. For most students, their primary school identity is, well, student. Their job is to be compliant, to understand what is expected of them, and to do the work—all for the reward of a grade. Teachers can provide what I call pseudohelp by providing rubrics that describe what needs to be in a piece of writing that is scored highly.

But this isn't how writing works outside the classroom. The issue is not about what writing has, but what writing does, and the effect it has on a reader. The driving force is not compliance but purpose, action, and the desire "to disturb the universe" (Eliot 1963, 3). This desire itself is rooted in our life stories, the complex of passions, beliefs, grievances, and life experiences we bring.

Liz works from the principle that all students have the life material to be writers, yet they need to reset their writerly self-regard. Teachers themselves need to write and share their own anxieties and missteps. And we all must confront the voices and cultural myths that trouble the sleep of even accomplished writers. After all, writing is about exposure, "putting yourself out there" as the saying goes—and we would be emotionally deficient if we were entirely calm about this. The question becomes, how can we use (or at least manage) the inevitable anxiety associated with writing and not be disabled by it?

Maybe the biggest trap is entitlement, that voice that says, *Who are* you *to want to write this? Don't you know that (a) it has been written about before; (b) there are better educated, more skilled, just plain smarter people out there who can do a better job than you; and (c) this is so obvious that no one will care?* Sound familiar?

In this book, Liz demystifies writing. Drawing on her own experience as a writer and teacher, and drawing extensively from writers' commentaries, she names the psychological impediments that inhibit even accomplished writers—perfectionism, procrastination, the imposter complex, memories of negative feedback, fear of failure, or steady negative self-talk. These, to some degree, go with the territory. But there are ways to mitigate them, and, for Liz, the primary way is to confront them through MetaWrites.

The *meta* refers to *metacognition*, thinking about our thinking. A major thread of this book is composed of invitations to write about writing. For example, she poses this question about writer's block:

> Contemporary novelist Jodi Picoult dismisses the idea of writer's block. "Think about it—when you were blocked in college and had to write a paper, didn't it always manage to fix itself the night before the paper was due? Writer's block is having too much time on your hands. If you have a limited amount of time to write, you just sit down and do it" (Charney 2017a). Do you agree or disagree that writer's block is just a matter of having too much time on your hands? What personal experience with writer's block informed your answer?

Or this one about perfectionism:

> Essayist Rebecca Solnit writes, "So many of us believe in perfection, which ruins everything else, because the perfect is not only the enemy of the good; it's also the enemy of the realistic, the possible, and the fun" (Gilbert 2015, 166). Do you agree or disagree with this statement? Do you or someone you know suffer from perfectionism? Has it ruined the real, the possible, and the fun you might have had with writing? Why or why not?

These prompts push students and teachers to write theory, to describe their experiences of writing, and as we all know, when we can name a fear, we are well on the way to dealing with it. Liz puts students in conversation with practicing writers. When we recognize that we are not alone in having inhibitions about writing and that others have ways of working through them, we can overcome the shame we feel in experiencing difficulty.

Liz names the mental obstacles that can invade the writing process. She invites us to join the ranks of the uncertain, the fearful, imposters all, creating texts that seem surer than we are. We will never be the mythological Writer, with Oz-like authority—but who would want that anyway? It's better to join the society of the fallible, who may struggle to talk down the demons, who fail but persist, who never feel comfortable claiming the title of writer, *but who write.*

Liz ends her book on this note of modesty:

> So here we are. The epilogue is written. I started this book not knowing exactly how the writing would work, but I performed the acts of writing until the writing emerged. . . . I acted like someone who is a writer.
>
> In short, I wrote *in doubt* and figured it out.

— Tom Newkirk

PART
ONE

The Case for Discovering Writing Identity & Developing Writing Courage

Writing Is
Hard

I teach about fifty student writers at Lafayette High School, a large, urban high school in Lexington, Kentucky. Students audition as eighth graders to get into the Literary Arts program, and we work together for four years on the art and craft of writing. It is, without a doubt, the most fulfilling professional job I've ever had.

When I was hired, I entertained certain notions about the students I would have—they would be gifted, creative, expressive, curious. Having now completed my tenth year, I can declare my students are all these things. Yet I discovered they also share something with all other students I've ever taught: a nagging doubt, a crippling fear, an overwhelming anxiety about their writing abilities.

Prior to coming to Lafayette, I taught in a range of English classes—reading intervention, collaborative English, Advanced Placement Lang, Advanced Placement Lit. I also taught composition and creative writing at Morehead State University, and for ten years, I was codirector of the Morehead Writing Project, working with teachers pursuing their master's.

With middle-aged teachers, undergraduates, or fifteen-year-old sophomores, the fears were the same. In every class I taught, I heard some version of "I'm not a good writer" or "I don't like to write" or "I don't have anything to write about." Yet, they all possessed the essentials to be a writer, to wit: thoughts about their life and a language to express those thoughts.

Of course, there's more to writing than that, but that's the start: an idea and the means to express it. Whether the writing is imaginative or rhetorical, the form, style, tone, and structure stems from that initial spark: I am a human who thinks, and I want to communicate something to another human in writing.

When I arrived at Lafayette, I figured I'd finally meet writers confident of their abilities. I wouldn't have to convince these students they had a story to tell. I wouldn't have to assure them they were good enough. They'd auditioned and gained acceptance into a gifted program for writers, after all.

Of course, I was wrong.

I heard all the moans and objections about writing from my gifted writers that I'd heard from everyone else, except with a larger degree of angsty melodrama: "I suck at writing." "My drafts are trash." "I don't even like to write."

In a 2019 survey of my incoming students, only 10 percent reported they felt confident as a writer. Sixty percent said they were somewhat confident as a writer. And a whopping 30 percent reported they were not confident as a writer. These kids had had many writing successes and had been told since elementary school they were gifted at written expression.

You could argue that trying to live up to the gifted label created these fears and doubts. You could argue their self-assessment was a sign of maturity or modesty or that they'd confused confidence with mastery. But the survey confirmed for me what I've often reckoned in my own writing life. Writing confidence is unstable. No matter how long you've practiced it, writing is an evolving skill that only a fool would claim to have mastered. That we use the word *mastery* to assess student writing is a disservice to the work of writing and a lie to students everywhere.

The bottom line: all writers struggle.

All Writers Struggle

Fear and struggle are twin companions of the writer. Disquiet is the constant reminder that you are, in fact, a writer. The fear of being exposed—of not being good enough, of not measuring up—is the writer's perennial writing partner.

In the 2019 Associated Writing Program conference keynote address, Colson Whitehead talked about his own uneasiness while working on *The Underground*

Railroad. Plucking Toni Morrison's *Beloved*, Edward P. Jones' *The Known World*, and Charles Johnson's *The Middle Passage* off his bookshelf, he settled in to "learn something from these great artists"(24). The result? "I was very glum for a time, and paralyzed. And then I told myself, no matter what you're writing about—slavery, or war, or family—someone smarter and more talented than you has already written about it" (24). If a two-time Pulitzer Prize winner is paralyzed and glum, is it any wonder our students approach the task of writing with less than gleeful enthusiasm?

When our school's writing committee decided to launch a writing lab, we wanted to find out about our students' attitudes about writing. We knew the research showed that positive writing attitudes decline as a student advances through middle and high school (Kear et al. 2000, 23). Lack of choice and positive feedback as well as the monotony and lack of self-expression associated with on-demand writing tests are cited as reasons for this decline. But we were also interested in what kinds of writing students were doing in school and out. In our survey (Figure 1–1), 366 students, grades 9 to 12, answered the survey and provided us with interesting data.

Sixty percent of the respondents were in some kind of accelerated English class. Fifty-two percent were most confident with narrative writing. Sixty-six percent were least confident with poetry. Thirty percent said they enjoyed writing, 15 percent said they didn't enjoy writing, and 55 percent said their enjoyment depended on what kind of writing they were doing.

Although the survey delivered what we expected in terms of attitudes about writing, it was still disheartening that so many students did not identify writing as a positive experience or identify themselves as writers, even though they indicated they were doing some form of writing in seven out of the eight classes they were enrolled in.

Frequency of participation often leads to the formation of identity. If you hike every day, you think of yourself as a hiker. If you commute to work, you're a commuter. But here were students who were participating in writing for nearly 88 percent of their classes but not identifying as a writer. The survey showed even students who enjoyed writing had their doubts about claiming an identity as a writer, evidence that there was a clear disconnect between doing and being.

Figure 1–1 ~ *Lafayette Writing Survey*

1. **In what grade are you currently?**

2. **In what English class are you currently enrolled?**

3. **In how many of your classes are you required to write?**

4. **How would you rate your confidence as a writer?**
   - ☐ I am very confident as a writer.
   - ☐ I am somewhat confident as a writer.
   - ☐ I am neither confident nor unconfident as a writer.
   - ☐ I am not confident as a writer.
   - ☐ I am very unconfident as a writer.

5. **What part(s) of the writing process are you confident in? (Check all that apply.)**
   - ☐ Coming up with good ideas to write about
   - ☐ Getting my ideas down on paper
   - ☐ Expressing and developing my ideas
   - ☐ Knowing how to arrange my ideas once they are down on paper
   - ☐ Visualizing an audience for my writing
   - ☐ Having a good vocabulary to express my ideas
   - ☐ Revising my writing (knowing what to take out and what to leave in for clarity)
   - ☐ Editing my writing (understanding how to apply the rules of spelling, capitalization, and grammar)
   - ☐ Finding a place to publish or perform my writing
   - ☐ Other

6. **What part(s) of the writing process are you least confident in? (Check all that apply.)**
   - ☐ Coming up with good ideas to write about
   - ☐ Getting my ideas down on paper
   - ☐ Expressing and developing my ideas
   - ☐ Knowing how to arrange my ideas once they are down on paper
   - ☐ Visualizing an audience for my writing
   - ☐ Having a good vocabulary to express my ideas

   - ☐ Revising my writing (knowing what to take out and what to leave in for clarity)
   - ☐ Editing my writing (understanding how to apply the rules of spelling, capitalization, and grammar)
   - ☐ Finding a place to publish or perform my writing
   - ☐ Other

7. **What form of writing are you the most confident in writing? (Check all that apply.)**
   - ☐ Poetry
   - ☐ Narrative (short story or personal narrative)
   - ☐ Argumentative (opinion or persuasive writing)
   - ☐ Informational (lab reports, summaries, historical reports, etc.)
   - ☐ Drama (stage play, screen play, video games, etc.)

8. **What form of writing are you not the least confident in writing? (Check all that apply.)**
   - ☐ Poetry
   - ☐ Narrative (short story or personal narrative)
   - ☐ Argumentative (opinion or persuasive writing)
   - ☐ Informational (lab reports, summaries, historical reports, etc.)
   - ☐ Drama (stage play, screen play, video games, etc.)

9. **Do you enjoy writing?**
   - ☐ Yes
   - ☐ No
   - ☐ Depends on what kind of writing it is

10. **Have you ever said any of the following about yourself as a writer? (Check all that apply.)**
    - ☐ I always have a lot of good ideas for writing.
    - ☐ I never have any good ideas for writing.
    - ☐ I am good at writing.
    - ☐ I am bad at writing.
    - ☐ I'm excited when other people read my writing.

- [ ] I'm afraid someone will make fun of me when they read my writing.
- [ ] I'm logical, so I'm not good at creative writing.
- [ ] I'm creative, so I'm not good at analytical writing.
- [ ] What I have to say matters.
- [ ] What I have to say doesn't matter.
- [ ] I am the best person to write about this topic.
- [ ] I am not the best person to write about this topic.

11. **Do you prefer writing for school assignments or for personal reasons?**
    - [ ] School assignments
    - [ ] Personal reasons
    - [ ] Neither school nor personal reasons

12. **At school, what kind of writing do you like to write? (Check all that apply.)**
    - [ ] Writing speeches
    - [ ] Writing argumentative essays
    - [ ] Writing stories
    - [ ] Writing blogs
    - [ ] Writing plays
    - [ ] Writing analytical essays
    - [ ] Writing novels
    - [ ] Writing songs
    - [ ] Writing poetry
    - [ ] Writing informational essays
    - [ ] Writing letters
    - [ ] Writing summaries
    - [ ] Writing lab reports
    - [ ] Writing in a journal from a prompt
    - [ ] Other

13. **Outside of school, what kind of writing do you like to write? (Check all that apply.)**
    - [ ] Writing speeches
    - [ ] Writing argumentative essays
    - [ ] Writing stories
    - [ ] Writing blogs

- [ ] Writing plays
- [ ] Writing analytical essays
- [ ] Writing novels
- [ ] Writing songs
- [ ] Writing poetry
- [ ] Writing informational essays
- [ ] Writing letters
- [ ] Writing summaries
- [ ] Writing lab reports
- [ ] Writing in a journal from a prompt
- [ ] Other

14. **What kind of writing would you like to learn more about either in school or outside school? (Check all that apply.)**
    - [ ] Writing speeches
    - [ ] Writing argumentative essays
    - [ ] Writing stories
    - [ ] Writing blogs
    - [ ] Writing plays
    - [ ] Writing analytical essays
    - [ ] Writing novels
    - [ ] Writing songs
    - [ ] Writing poetry
    - [ ] Writing informational essays
    - [ ] Writing letters
    - [ ] Writing summaries
    - [ ] Writing lab reports
    - [ ] Other

15. **What was your best writing experience, either in school or outside of school?**

16. **What was your worst writing experience, either in school or outside of school?**

17. **What three words describe you as a writer?**

One of the most heartbreaking results of the survey were the answers to #17, "What three words describe you as a writer?" More than a quarter of respondents answered with something negative:

Bad at it

Not very good

Not a writer

Bad at writing

I don't know.

Maybe they thought writing talent was a gift given to the chosen few, a divine bestowal. Or perhaps they didn't see themselves as writers because they'd never published anything or won any prizes. Or didn't see their process as one that produced the kind of writing—neat, orderly, sitting on a library shelf—they associated with being a writer. They sensed their stumbling efforts didn't match up. Maybe they hadn't been told yet that struggle and stumbling was an essential part of the process.

Dismantling the Myth of the Master Writer

To be honest with students about the struggle of writing might scare them off, but it's more ethical than advancing, even unconsciously, the myth of the master writer. Anne Lamott (1994) describes this myth as writers who "sit down at their desks every morning feeling like a million dollars, feeling great about who they are and how much talent they have and what a great story they have to tell; that they take a few deep breaths, push back their sleeves, roll their necks a few times to get all the cricks out and dive in, typing fully formed passages as fast as a court reporter" (52).

When I was about seventeen, I saw a television special on romance author Danielle Steel, who, according to *Forbes* (2021), has published over 170 books in the last forty years. In full-face makeup, a coiffed updo, and pink pant suit, Steel sat down at a gilded table in her spacious Parisian office.

With a manicured hand, she slid a piece of paper in her Olympia standard typewriter and began "Flight of the Bumblebee" typing. We cut away to an interview with her, then when the scene resumed, Steel pulled the paper out of the typewriter and laid it on top of a stack of similarly typed papers, which, presumably, was the finished manuscript of her next novel ready to be shipped off to her publisher.

A writer that knows exactly what to say and how to say it is often the image our students have of what a writer is supposed to be. This mirage has the trappings of privilege, leisure, education, plus long stretches of time to spend writing. Recently my student Kate wrote about this fantasy in her notebook: "I always pictured a writer as someone who would wake up in the morning, make a cup of coffee, and curl up with an old-fashioned typewriter in a cozy blanket by the fireplace and tap away at the typewriter all day."

This concept of The Master Writer is pervasive in popular culture, yet at odds with the struggle involved in bringing forth even the most basic of drafts. In my process, there's a lot of pacing, staring out the window, and wasting time. Even some groaning and wringing of hands. Writing makes me feel isolated in my own incompetence, but it's a practice I submit to over and over because the results are rewarding. Most of our students don't experience the reward that offsets the struggle. To them, writing is torture, and the result is shame.

The Master Writer myth began to crack for me when I pursued a Master's in Fine Arts degree in fiction. I worked closely for three years with very talented writers, and their struggles, habits, and self-loathing mirrored my own. We had a robust visiting writers series, and all the visiting writers, many legends of American letters, recounted stories of writing frustrations as well.

My MFA colleagues and I had a writing identity. Whitehead and all those writers in Murray's book also had an identity that helped them forge past the anxiety and fear that accompanies writing. However, for the students who do not have one, when the words don't flow and their fingers don't magically play over the Chromebook, they may believe they don't have what it takes to write at all. Maybe they think writers are born, not made.

When there's a misconception about how writers work, students misinterpret the normal struggle as part of their own damage. And especially if they look around the classroom where everyone else seems to be merrily typing away.

Why Teaching Fortitude to Support Writing Identity Is Necessary

We rarely talk about the social-emotional resilience needed around the act of writing. I've always been fascinated about how important identity is to the development of literacy skills, yet how infrequently identity is addressed or discussed in the classroom.

Think about what we ask of students when we ask them to write: look inside your life and yank out a significant event, interpret that event, and then communicate its implications with clarity to a make-believe audience. Or form an opinion strong enough to argue a claim while building credibility, weaving in research, and touching the hearts and minds of nameless, faceless readers. And if the technical demands of writing aren't hard enough to master, we're also asking them to forge past the voices in their heads saying *You're a bad writer*.

All these tasks require more than just knowing the rules of writing. They require agency, writerly decision making, an authoritative stance. They require, in short, a consciousness separate from school and teacher, an autonomy born from self-identity and social identity and from their ability to make effective writing happen. In short, they require a writing identity.

Think about how different the year would be for students if we started by asking students not just "Who are you?" but "Who are you as a writer?" That question taps a self-concept, letting students know you already regard them as writers, yet you're asking them to skill up their writing game. For this reason, teaching students their fears are normal and even necessary during the writing process is not only important, but essential. Teaching students strategies to subjugate their fears in the service of their writing goals is giving them not only the gift of fortitude, but a means to define, expand, and declare their writing identity.

"Trying to deny, avoid, numb, or eradicate the fear of writing is neither possible nor desirable," writes Ralph Keyes (1995) in *The Courage to Write*. "Anxiety is not only an inevitable part of the writing process but a necessary part. A state of anxiety is the writer's natural habitat" (13). The goal, then, is not to master the anxiety or shutter the fear, but to learn to write *with* the fear and anxiety present. When students have practiced this over and over—feeling the fear that writing produces and overcoming it with healthy strategies—their writing identity soars, and they are fortified to face the next writing task with a greater degree of independence and power.

It's essential to have anxiety when you write, just as it is essential to be nervous before you go on stage. In this sense, the page is a kind of stage where students perform as a writer. If an actor doesn't feel nervous and keyed up before the lights go up, the performance will be flat. Yes, stage fright can be debilitating, but the positive energy of excitement and anticipation gives a stage performance its vitality. Our goal is to help students harness what Keyes calls "the power of positive anxiety" (14) in a way that augments their writing, not diminishes it.

When I conceived this book, I struggled with my main aim: Am I arguing for the necessity of teaching courage to students or am I arguing for the necessity of teaching writing identity? Midway through writing the first draft, I discovered the answer was *Yes!* Writing courage is necessary for discovering one's writing identity, and writing identity generates tenacity. The two states are interdependent.

Students who have a writing identity are just as likely to fall prey to the fears that beset students who are only writing for a grade, but they have a greater fortitude to write *with* the fears instead of letting the fears shut down the process. The more students recognize their identity as a writer, the greater degree of control they have over the writing fears that formerly would have sidetracked their goals. Because they write from ownership and not from compliance, writing becomes a pronouncement of self onto the world, a reward larger than any grade on a report card. Developing a writing identity helps to shift writing away from a teacher-directed activity to a student-pursued one that lasts a lifetime. Here are four more reasons teaching writing courage and writing identity are powerful.

Students Feel Less Isolated

Truth telling about one's own experience is liberating to all those who identify and see their own struggle in that truth. If we share our own stories of writing anxiety, this admission allows our students to relax. It's OK. It's normal. Teaching kids courage to write their stories will liberate and invite the shyest, most timid voice.

In my first book, I wrote about an activity I use in my classroom called Firepit, where we sit around a construction paper fire in the middle of the room and tell stories (Prather 2017, 50). It's one of the single best things I do. Kids tell funny, heroic, embarrassing stories about themselves. The shyest person in the room sees the fears she treasures up in her heart are not solely her own, but property everyone in the room owns. She feels less alone, less isolated. Talking about our own writing fears, sharing our anxieties, and reading about published authors crippled by years of writer's block or devastated by rejection helps a student understand these fears are *part of* being a writer.

When I share my writing process with students, I show them drafts of articles or blogs I've written to illustrate that writing is a hard and rocky. Two years ago I wrote a feature article about a local sportscaster for *Kentucky Living* magazine (Prather 2018). I brought in my interview notes, my research notes, and nine drafts I had printed out to show students the vast differences between the first and last draft. I also shared my process, describing how the first two drafts were wooden and "list-y," just one fact after the other. Sharing that I had no clue how to organize the piece helped students see that initial confusion was legitimate and realistic, not evidence that the writer is flawed. Sharing my frustrations normalized their anxiety.

Students Take the Necessary Risks

Living authentically is risky. Thinking is risky. Standing up for what you believe in, going against the crowd, taking a stand—all these virtues we want to cultivate in our students start with courage. And all these things are necessary for writing too. Speaking truth instead of relying on clichés or speaking plainly instead of ironically requires a risk. And anywhere there is risk, bravery is a must.

Teaching courage may sound very touchy-feely, like asking students to practice trust falls off cafeteria tables. But there's nothing touchy-feely about students examining, for example, the logic of a long-held belief about themselves or about the world. In fact, this kind of investigation requires focus and will. This kind of examination requires questioning everything, possibly rejecting the beliefs of a parent or someone they love. That's where the risk lies: in alienating themselves and others by examining a belief that might crumble upon intense scrutiny. That's why developing writing identity and nerve is essential.

Taking risks is the essence of writing. Putting a thought down for someone else to read exposes you in a way not many other activities do. If we want to sustain students in this process of writing, teaching courage comes first. Student writers who become more authentic in their writing risk exposure, but speaking their truth is worth it. In addition, they become part of a larger community of writers who also face the same fears.

Students Tell Their Own Story

I want my students to write their stories before someone else does. To challenge stereotypes. To speak in their own voice and language. Developing that voice starts with an embrace of their own identity and intentional instruction on writing bravely.

In an economically poor but culturally rich state like Kentucky, some students think their own culture is deficient or nonexistent. Some of them are aware that their story has been co-opted by outsiders who attempt to interpret and explain our state and its culture. Writing is a means of taking back that power because writing *is* power. As Kentucky writer Robert Gipe (2019) observed in a recent writing conference, "In Appalachia, people narrate their way into the meaning of their lives." Courage to write their own story is an essential practice for students who live in these underrepresented populations. They must write their own story, getting the details true to their own experience, especially if that vision challenges a stereotype.

Students Honor Their Selfhood

Every writing teacher recognizes students who have forged an identity for themselves. Some may call it a quality of voice; some may call it flow, but it is the boldness with which a writer steps onto the page, the authority with which she speaks a truth. It's a sure-footed progression of thought. It's a pronouncement of personality, of selfhood.

As a writer with identity grows and encounters different writing tasks, he faces these tasks independently and owns them more deeply. When I ask students who don't have a writing identity why they are writing something, they will say, "Because you told me to" or "Because it was assigned" or "IDK." When I ask my students in conferences, "Why are you writing this?" students who own their work and see their work as personally satisfying will tell me. They say things like, "Remember that short story we read last year where the bank robber shoots the guy, and as the bullet goes through his brain, he remembers his whole life? I'm trying to do something like that." Or "I follow this Instagram called 'Humans of New York' and I want to interview people here at school and find out their stories and call it 'Humans of Lafayette.'"

Writing identity creates ownership and voice, which starts with self. When you help students find strategies to manage their anxiety, you give them the freedom to declare the truth about who they are and what they believe.

What Is Writing Identity?

In this book, we will explore the idea of writing identity, but briefly defined, it is the merging of a student's social and self-identity with her writerly self-regard (Figure 1–2). That last element—writerly self-regard—is key. It is a student's ability, as my student Karsten said, "to know your way around a piece of writing." It's the degree to which students value their own abilities or esteem their own choices over the choices of others. It's a student's awareness that her life, voice, stories, points of view, sense of humor, memories, style of writing, vocabulary, syntactical choices, and organizational strategies are primary when she approaches any writing task.

Writerly self-regard is fluid and also relational in that it connects both to how you see yourself as a writer and also to the act of writing. From an educational standpoint, it's the most elastic. It's a student's belief he can make independent writing decisions that result in both effective and ineffective writing and maybe not die from it. It's a multifaceted construct that captures everything a writer brings with him when he picks up a pen, including his mentors and influences, his healthy and unhealthy writing habits and attitudes, his positive and negative writing experiences, and his emotions about the act of writing and himself as a writer.

Figure 1–2 ~ *The Elements of Writing Identity*

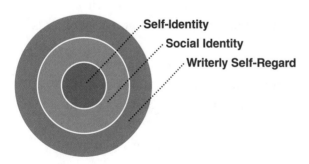

- Self-Identity
- Social Identity
- Writerly Self-Regard

Of course, if a student has low self-regard, it will be difficult to forge writerly self-regard, but not impossible. In fact, centering a student's selfhood in his writing will do both simultaneously. Writerly self-regard is the element that I, as a writing teacher, want to serve as a catalyst for. I want my classroom to be the place where writerly self-regard is centered, to support students' belief that their voices and skill sets can deliver their aims effectively. We will spend the rest of this book ruminating on these ideas, but let me briefly break down these three elements of writing identity with a single student, Zoya, as an illustration.

Self-Identity

As a writer, our sense of self or selfhood is formed by how we define who we are. Self-identity is the inner place of our core values, attitudes, and beliefs about ourselves and the world. Psychologically, our sense of self emerges from our belief system, our memories, and our experiences. And these are largely formed by our parents and family, our background and neighborhood, maybe even our faith system. One's perception of self is the oldest and often most concretized of the identities that will be brought into the service of writing, even as it shifts and grows through childhood, adolescence, young adult, adult, and so on.

Here's how Zoya, a ninth grader in my Literary Arts 1 class, described herself: "The first thing that comes to mind is my heritage. My Indian nationality and Asian ethnicity are the biggest parts of my self-identity. Secondly, my identity as an immigrant is also very important to me because it is a part of my identity that I interact with the most. Along with that, my role as a woman, a teenager, and a student are a part of my self-identity."

As a social construct, Zoya's self-identity is fluid and progressive yet has properties, such as her heritage and autobiographical memories, that are stable. It's the deep, soul seat from which she as a writer will step into the world. Her story begins with who she sees herself to be.

Social Identity

A writer's social identity is constructed by the groups we participate in, formed primarily but not solely by our socioeconomic status, our race or ethnicity, our gender, our sexual orientation. Another fluid social construct, social identity sets us in relation to other people, deposits us inside and outside communities, and follows both the social, cultural, and political changes we experience throughout our lives.

Social identity might also be formed by our culture, the geographical place we come from or currently live in, or the clubs and organizations that we have joined. Social identity is the awareness of ourselves as a self within a community within a world.

Zoya writes, "I consider myself a part of several social groups. My culture as Indian and the religions I grew up around, Hinduism and Islam. My status as an immigrant. Along with those, I am a progressive, so I align with the Democratic party. In school, I am a part of academic groups and my creative writing class. Lastly, my affiliation with the agnostic religion is also very prominent in my social identity."

Interestingly, awareness of what groups we're a part of, what groups we reject, and what groups reject us is a powerful and never-ending well of writing fodder. Think of all the great personal narratives that boil down to "I once thought I was an X, but now I realize I am a Y, and here's what I've discovered from that journey."

Writerly Self-Regard

Writerly self-regard rounds out the triad of elements and is the most important. It's the fuel that drives the car of writing identity. Formed from the writer's writing experiences and their skills and attitude toward writing, writerly self-regard is the element that teachers and a writing classroom can influence the most profoundly.

Zoya writes: "My identity as a writer has grown a lot over the years. While I started off as an amateur poet and short story author, I have grown into a more serious and mature writer. I have taken on the role of an opinion journalist and screenplay writer, both roles have affected my writing persona in their own ways. Unfortunately, I am also a 'procrast-writer' or a writer who delays writing down any ideas they might have into actual writing. As bad as that is, it is still very important to my identity as a writer."

Already Zoya has witnessed and claimed an identity as a writer that names several modes she likes to write and takes into account a delay mechanism that is part of her process. Although she understands that procrastination might be an unhealthy practice, it *is* part of who she is as a writer at the present moment in her development.

The successes and practices in a writing community, such as one formed in an ELA classroom, are foundational in developing a student's writerly self-regard. In a classroom where student voice is centered, a writer's level of skill can also be amplified and healthy habits exercised. Students can also participate in giving and receiving feedback, discover peer mentors, and practice rhetorical problem-solving as a collaborative, inquiry-based process. All these activities strengthen students' writerly self-regard, which strengthens their larger writing identity.

How to Use This Book

Every writing task is a puzzle with complex problems to solve. By the time a student reaches the sixth grade, she should have been introduced to and practiced the basic technical, grammatical, and mechanical knowledge to be a writer. From that point on, writing is an ongoing practice of cracking new rhetorical and narrative problems in the form of assigned and self-selected writing tasks. (Eighty percent of the writing tasks in my class are self-selected, and 20 percent are assigned.) Writing instruction from seventh to twelfth grade, then, should be hundreds of low-stakes puzzle opportunities to practice, practice, practice coupled with a number of larger student-directed projects that run from conception to publication.

Because writing is a skill taught in school, it is erroneously perceived by many students as an academic performance rather than a representation of self. But thinking, reading, and writing are not purely academic pursuits any more than breathing, running, and walking are purely athletic pursuits. A student with an awareness of her own writing identity moves beyond mere slavish compliance to an academic grade and finds an entry point even on a state-issued assessment. During middle and high school, a student's identity as a writer begins to change and takes on greater postures of autonomy. Writing identity becomes both a grounding wire and launching pad for every writing task, from a business proposal to a research paper to a love note to an Instagram post.

This book is designed to help students launch into a rich self-investigation by naming and examining their writing identity through practical writing activities.

Several of them are included in the appendixes as reproducible copies to use with your classes. They have no special order and could be used at any time during the school year. Think of these as an analytical, social-emotional curriculum that augments your existing instruction. I use most of these exercises during the first six weeks of my school year to lay the groundwork for conversations we'll continue having all year. The concept of writing identity—specifically asking students to make their own writerly decisions and to do the hard work around writing production—is a running undercurrent in our writing community that allows me to get to know my student writers.

You'll notice short writing prompts about writing throughout, called MetaWrites, some designed for teachers and some for students. By examining our own writing experiences, we will be in a place to share and reflect those lessons with our students. These prompts ask a writer to (a) pay attention to the practice of writing by (b) writing about (c) the practice of writing itself. You may write with your students during these MetaWrites to be vulnerable and to connect through the shared experience of writing, but there's no expectation to share what you write with anyone unless you want to. You may want to share some of your insights with your students, either in readings, conversations, or demonstrations, or you may not.

Here in Chapter 1, I briefly define writing identity and argue that teaching writing courage is an essential part of any ELA classroom. In Chapters 2, 3, and 4, I dive into writing identity proper, providing tools to help teachers and students unpack their writing history to address any residual narratives that no longer serve their growth. In these chapters, teachers and students also claim their habits, mentors, and ideas as the social and emotional capital from which they write. These examinations lay the groundwork for the kind of vulnerability, reflection, and personal exploration helpful in declaring a writing identity.

Chapter 3 is mostly targeted toward the ELA teacher who teaches, among dozens of other things, writing. Knowing yourself as a writer and knowing how you process writing tasks will be critical when conferencing with students, for example, or when you help them solve a particularly knotty rhetorical problem. Examining the kinds of assumptions, preconceptions, injuries, and thrills you experienced as a writer in elementary through high school will help you develop a personal philosophy around writing and writing instruction. Sharing stories about your own writing identity and your approach to writing tasks creates an authentic communal experience with your students.

In Chapters 5, 6, and 7, we name the monsters that threaten to shut down the identity of the writer. By naming and disarming our fears—imposter syndrome, perfectionism, procrastination, and so on—we provide students strategies they can use the rest of their lives. We break down those logjams in a few ways: we write about them, of course; we try to name how these obstructions feel and where they come from emotionally; we give ourselves permission and grace to remember and analyze how we have overcome them in the past; and we look at how professional writers experience these same barriers and use these anxieties to fuel their work.

PART TWO

Discovering Writing Identity

Forging
a Writing Identity
by Writing

This book is dedicated to two of my high school English teachers, Sharon Toadvine and Lynda Umfress. They represent the Alpha and Omega of my formative writing identity, the yin and yang of why I am a writer today.

I went to a small rural high school in Bourbon County, Kentucky. There were 144 kids in my graduating class; we had small class sizes, passionate teachers, and committed administrators. I matriculated during a sweet spot in education history, just as the National Commission on Excellence in Education's *A Nation at Risk* (1983) flung the whole nation into rigor panic, but not before classrooms shifted to put the deeply problematic report into practice.

Mrs. Toadvine was my Freshman English teacher. Young, tan, and idealistic, she told us on the first day of class we were required to keep a daily writing journal. No one had ever asked us to do this before. It was a startling notion. I don't remember if there were prompts. I don't remember much of anything about that year except this: I was fourteen and someone had asked me to write down my thoughts.

Every week I wrote down the events of my life, and, on the weekends, she wrote back:

It sounds like you've been doing a lot of thinking about yourself.

I have confidence in you. You'll be all right! You're human—don't be too hard on yourself.

Whatever else you may believe, please believe that I care about you. You are a special person.

She responded to each student in green ink on three-by-five-inch index cards that she stapled into our notebooks. Sensible, efficient, kind. How did she keep up with it? A saint among teachers.

One night as I sat at the kitchen table, scribbling in my notebook, my mother said to me: "You know, your teacher's probably reading that to the other teachers in the teachers lounge, and they're laughing at you." It was incredibly cruel, intended to shame and stop me from writing down my life, but it had the opposite effect.

"Really?!" I said. *An audience!* I thought, delighted.

The next year, I signed up for a journalism class and met another teacher, Ms. Umfress, who served as my mentor for the next three years on our student newspaper staff. She taught me lessons in clarity, audience, and word economy that I use to this day. Upon graduation, I decided to major in English in college and have been a writer for the last forty years.

When Mrs. Toadvine asked me to write from my life, using my voice, about things that mattered to me, writing became part of who I was and how I processed life. And when Ms. Umfress asked me to declare my thoughts to a larger audience in the form of a newspaper article, I moved into another level of identity. Both teachers were essential to the formation of my writerly self-regard. Mrs. Toadvine gave me the safety and freedom to develop my voice and speak my truth; Ms. Umfress gave me an understanding of rhetorical situation and how to speak that truth to a wider audience. Student writers need both these kinds of teachers multiple times in their life.

The poems I scribbled on cast-off utility bill envelopes, the stories I wrote on the backs of church bulletins, the letters I wrote to my grandmothers: these were part of that identity too. You might say I was primed to respond to Mrs. Toadvine's invitation because I already thought like a writer or because I had some writing talent. But we will never know if that's true. She did offer me that outlet and changed my life.

Of course there is more to writing identity than having two teachers who encouraged writing in their classrooms, but that's where it started for me. When I saw that my words made a difference—that I could make people laugh and think and cry and take action—that was power.

Centering the Student

I'm the youngest of five children, born to a World War II vet and a homemaker, raised on a tobacco and cattle farm in central Kentucky. I'm a Taurus, an Ennea-gram 3, an INFJ, and a Gen Xer. I am married with no children, drive a Honda, vote in every election, and have fifty-two varieties of daylilies in my backyard. I could use the rest of this chapter to claim categories of belonging where my social and self-identity reside, but the point is when I sit down to write, all of these selves come with me. My obsessions, my history, my memory, and my emotions are all there.

Everything I have read is there too, bubbling under the surface, and everything I have experienced, positively and negatively, is stored somewhere in a lobe or a wrinkle. All these elements contribute to my writing identity, which is both fixed and flexible. My autobiography is mostly fixed, even as I revisit and revise its meaning. My skill level is mostly flexible, as I grow as a writer and gain more skill.

Helping students discover their writing identity starts with centering all the obsessions and passions and topics and history that they bring with them. Allow-ing students to write about their own life, using their own language, to find and amplify their own voice is where identity formation starts. Writing, then, becomes more about meaning making and truth telling than about getting it right and getting it done. Writing becomes an activity that is personal, revelatory, and meaningful.

Here's the problem: many students feel like they have to be someone other than who they really are to be a good writer. They often perceive that writing requires not their language and not their style to be successful. Instead of seeing writing as a means of expression that originates and is controlled entirely by them, writing is perceived as task that is imposed on them by someone else who dictates the aims, the value, and the production of the task.

Be aware that asking some students to identify as a writer feels like a trap. They may not feel like identifying as a writer because, in school where they do most of their writing, someone else makes the decisions on the topic, the form, and the audience for them. They may have no agency or autonomy from which to enter a writing task. They also may not identify as a writer because they may hate writing or hate school or hate their writing teacher, and they see identifying as a writer as connected to all those things. Instead of understanding that a writing identity is connected to their self, their ambitions, their passions, they may think that identifying as a writer means getting good grades or being praised by a teacher.

Here's a nuance to ponder: it will be beyond some students to *identify* as writers but they should understand they do possess a writing *identity* that is built from their self-identity/social identity and all their writing experiences and skills. Students can understand and appreciate their own writing identities without having to declare that they love writing or love to write, which is a sure invitation for defeat and hypocrisy. I often don't love writing or love to write, but I value and respect the act. I understand and appreciate its power in my life and in the world.

I want to cultivate in my students the awareness that writing—thinking on the page—is a power tool to be used for the rest of their lives. In every aspect of their lives, not just college and career, students can record their histories, understand their past, process personal and world events, and maintain equilibrium in turbulent times.

Last week during a Zoom, I asked my juniors this exact question: "What do you think the difference is between having a writing identity and identifying as a writer?"

"Identifying as a writer is kind of like when someone has a job writing, like what you do," said Emma. "But your writing identity is kind of like who you are on the page, your persona when you write and your approach to writing. Like, your style."

"Yes," I said. "Persona does seem to be part of that."

"It's easier to identify as a writer," Sarah said.

"Really? That's interesting. Tell me why."

"Literally anyone can just say, 'I'm a writer.'"

"Yeah, having a writing identity, to me, is more specific to yourself. Like how *you* write and the experiences *you've* been through that affected your writing and how it's unique to you," Walker said.

"Same," said Sarah. "Writing identity is what you write, you know, what genre you like to write, the voice you use."

As a teacher, I want to tread lightly here: my goal is to help student writers elevate and value the identity that makes them unique while helping them gain technical skill. Nothing about their self-identity or social identity needs to be changed to write; my goal is to only deepen and broaden their writerly self-regard through practice and learning writing technique.

I often use an "already/not yet" paradox to explain to students how they *already* possess the self-identity and social identity where their writing comes from but they may *not yet* have fully grasped all the skill they need. Before I wrote my first book, I *already* had a writing identity, but had *not yet* learned the skill of producing a book-length volume of writing. Just because students don't *yet* have a handle on grammar doesn't mean they haven't *already* felt something so deep and so profound that they want to write about it. This paradox is hard to assess, but it's critical for a student's growing writerly regard. When a student might *not yet* understand how to organize her thoughts, she *already* has something to say and a language to say it with.

Here's an example of the already/not yet paradox in living color: I once sponsored our high school literary journal, *The Laurel*. Any student at our school could submit a piece of writing in a bin outside my door, attaching a cover letter with all the pertinent contact information.

One day we got a submission, but the writer had not attached a cover letter, and there were no identifying marks on it at all.

"Listen to this," said my managing editor Serena, who read it out loud.

It was a love letter, but it was unlike anything we'd ever read. The speaker was apologizing for cheating and his awareness of breaking a trust and the loss of a love he would never recover from. There was not one cliché in the whole letter. It was so fresh and original, but nearly unreadable due to so many misspelled words and grammatical errors. Serena sat down and typed up the letter, correcting all the mangled grammar, fragments, and misspelled words. With all the original language and her tidy edits, it was a beauty.

"We can't publish that," our executive editor said. "We don't know who wrote it, and it's not a good piece of writing."

"It's a great piece of writing," Serena said. "Were you listening?"

Several other students in the room chimed in: What makes a piece of writing good? Who was the real writer: Serena, who had written the sentences correctly, or the unknown author, who had written something with such sincerity and voice as to astonish us all?

Of course, the "real" writer was the unknown student. It was *his* identity that made those fresh, arresting choices, it was *his* cognition that selected those startling, clear details of *his* infidelity. Serena had only edited his work; she hadn't created it.

This is an example of a student who *already* had a purpose, a form, an audience, and something original to say but had *not yet* mastered the conventions of standard English to achieve his aims. I tell this story to my students to say that only they can tell their story. Even though others may edit it, teachers may grade it, editors may revise it, only they can create it. From their mind, with their voice, for their own ends. The heart and soul of writing comes from them.

Changing the Language We Use to Talk About Writing

One way to have this conversation with students is to examine the language we use when we talk about writing. I want my students to reject the moralizing binary of good and bad and embrace more writing-based questions: What are the aims of the storyteller? What is working? What is the purpose of this piece of writing? Is this introduction effective for my aims?

I also hope students reject the binary between emotions versus logic if they have internalized the academic preference that argumentative writing is somehow superior to narrative. I don't want students to unconsciously suppress a narrative urge, for example, to elevate what they might perceive as the superiority of argumentation. By doing so, students' intellectual and emotional tools are cut in half when they attempt to bring forth any type of writing. So we ask the questions: How does the author achieve her purpose? What are her aims?

"Who cares about any of these questions? What do they have to do with us?" a student might ask. These questions go to the heart of writing identity and how we think about ourselves as writers fundamentally informs the process by which we write. If the student perceives the writing as good or bad, then maybe the person who wrote it is also good or bad.

Assignations of "good" and "bad" and "real" and "not real" diminish the conversation we have around writing growth and writing identity. If a student conceives of himself as a bad writer, he has limited his work and his potential for growth. And, of course, it's only a few mental steps from "I'm a bad writer" to "I'm a bad student" or "I am bad."

Students who possess a writing identity—not identifying as a good or bad writer—have a greater hardiness for facing the ups and downs of the writing process. They begin to understand that all writers—those on the bestseller list and those sitting right next to them in the classroom—suffer and succeed in same proportions during the process. Students who engage healthily with writing are more committed to the process than with just turning something in. They have more autonomy and participate in greater writerly decisions than a student who just writes for the limited rewards of a grade.

Even though these kinds of definitions serve no purpose in learning, we continue to assign value to writing and writers when we talk about mentor texts, as in "Is this a good piece of writing?" instead of "Is this an effective piece of writing?" This small tweak subconsciously informs students how to think about their own work in those terms as well.

Students have a lot to say about this.

"How do you know if you're a real writer or not?" Samantha asked when we had finished doing an opening writing prompt.

"I'm not sure what you mean," I said, dying a little inside because I'd spent all of the previous two days attempting to eradicate assignations of "real" writers and "not real" writers.

"There's no such thing as a real writer." Marley, a sophomore, looked up from the corner of the room. She'd been playing with her phone most of the class period, so I wasn't even sure she was listening. "Each person has the ability to write, but it's those that have the courage to have their voices heard are seen with the label of writer." She air quoted *writer*. "This 100 percent applies to me. I did not write at all last year."

"I thought you couldn't go around declaring that you were a writer unless you had work published to prove it," said Samantha.

"There's a difference between being a writer and being an author," my peer tutor Michael cut in. Intense and idealistic with a mop of curly black hair and a talent for writing far beyond his years, he led them in writing activities that generated many of their writing ideas. Earlier in the year, after we had witnessed a total eclipse of the sun, for example, he led them in an opening freewrite: Write about your experience of the eclipse.

"This writing can be about a description of who you were with, what you did, how you felt about the eclipse, anything. And we'll write for about seven minutes," Michael explained.

I settled in the back of the room to write. My freewrite was a funny little anecdote of how our faculty congregated on the school's front lawn, playing music, munching on MoonPies, and drinking Sunkist. I looked around my room. Twenty-seven students, heads bent over their notebooks, scritching and scratching their experience.

"OK time's up. Who wants to share?"

Crickets. It was, after all, only the seventh day of school. Everyone was new to everyone else, and it was a big class.

"I'll go," I said. "I'll share," thinking if I read my funny little ditty, it would be easier for someone else to go.

"Well . . ." Michael paused, then laughed in his casual, dismissive way. "I wanted a real writer to share."

All eyes on me.

For a split second, my reflexive ego kicked up, saying things egos always say: not a real writer, not a real teacher, shouldn't even be responsible for watching children. Just as quickly, I realized what he meant. Of course, he wanted one of the students to share.

"Fair enough," I laughed. "Let a *real* writer share."

The class went on. Someone shared, then another, and another. They were delightful tales of making eclipse cookies, of demon babies being conceived, and missing the eclipse because of naps.

Later I thought about my reaction, an involuntary response from some deeply held fear of exposure that I'm not a real writer, that my work isn't good enough, that I'm a fake. I don't believe I'm alone in this kind of fear, and I know my students, who have much less experience with writing success than I do, have these thoughts all the time. These thoughts form students' inner dialogue with themselves and sometimes they make their way into spoken negations. When we have feedback workshops, I have made a rule: no apologies; no negative self-talk. Otherwise, it's five minutes of throat clearing and apologies from the writer under consideration to make sure we know that they know that this piece is "trash." They fortify themselves against the possibility that we will think of them as a "bad" writer by beating us to the punch.

The blow to a young writer's identity can be unconsciously dealt and not malicious, so the words we use to describe writing and writers are important. It's also important to start with some foundational conversations.

Four Activities That Lead to Foundational Conversations

Within the first week or two of school, we'll do one or two of the following activities that generate some of the most important conversations we have all year. These conversations lay the groundwork for writing a literacy narrative or a philosophy of writing essay, two pieces of writing I often open the year with.

By asking students to write about their own writing, I also gather anecdotal data on my students' prior experiences with writing. All these experiences impact the writing they do in my class, so I want to educate myself on that background. For example, some have the idea that writing for school and writing in other areas of life bear no resemblance to each other; others have been taught that there is a static, predictable process all writing goes through to a finished draft. Some believe the purpose of writing is only the transmission of facts or opinions, but not a means of discovering facts and opinions. All of them have experiences with the act of writing, and those experiences often mirror the realities of professional writers. With these activities, I'm interested in shaking the notion that there are good writers and bad writers or that writing is a gift only the supernatural possess.

Tracking Identity with Circles, Charts, and Maps

A great opening day activity is to ask students to declare their different identities, including their writing identity. This activity may be difficult for some students who have never considered having a writing identity, but I model the process on the board before we get started, and we have some fun making up edgy names for our identities.

Students draw three circles in their writing notebook and divide each circle into eight pie slices. In the first circle, students write one word or phrase on each of the pie slices that describes their self-identity. In the second pie, students write words that describe their social identity. In the third pie, students write words that describe who they are as a writer.

For example, Zoya wrote in her social circle: "teenager, student, immigrant, agnostic, Bengali, daughter, dog person, and only child." In her self circle, she wrote "middle-class, Indian, she/her, writer, straight/cisgender, singer, progressive." And in her writer circle, she wrote "angry feminist, proud ally, hopeless romantic, and won't-back-down liberal."

My colleague Venecia Proctor developed a chart to help her students track the different overlay of identities that form their writing identity. She tells her students, "Is there a difference between the you you are inside and the you you project to the world? How do these identities reveal themselves in your writing?" Figure 2–1 is designed to gather some data around how her students' social and self-identities combine with their writing experiences to form their writing identity.

Creating a map—tracking the progression or the path of one's writing journey—is another reflection activity that offers up a lot of great conversations. Different from Georgia Heard's "heart maps" and Nanci Atwell's "writing territories" that both map out areas, people, and events in students' lives that they may want to write about, these maps invite students to actually track the progression of their own writing literacy, to map their awareness of growing as a writer.

When my students started mapping their own writing identity, they also began to track the stories and moments of their lives that created their writing philosophy. One day we shared some of the events from their maps.

In remembering when she started to think about her argumentative style, Sarah Grace said, "My parents said I couldn't claim to believe something unless I explained why I believed it. I think I was four years old when they started that."

"My dad would tell us bedtime stories, but at some point, he would just start them and I would take over and finish them," Griffin said. "And then I started just telling bedtime stories to myself and my brother."

"When I got to school and everyone could write and I couldn't, I realized it was something I wanted to do," Regan said. She pointed to a tiny schoolhouse with a book hovering overhead on her map.

Kennedy pointed to a large doll she'd drawn on her map. "When I was in second grade, everyone struggled to write, but I didn't and I entered a story into a story contest, and I won an American Girl Doll (it was Kit), so I figured out early that writing could get me certain things."

Figure 2–1 ~ *What Makes Up Your Writing Identity?*

Your writing identity is made up of several things: who you identify as, the communities you identify with, and how you see yourself as a writer. When you sit down to write, you bring with you a combination of these identities. The chart below breaks down these elements to help you think about your writing identity.

Instructions: Describe your identities in the blank row below.

Self-Identity	Social Identity	Writerly Self-Regard
Describe how you see yourself: race/ethnicity, personality type, values, beliefs, attitudes, memories, gender, birth order, age, grade level or education.	*Describe the groups you are a part of: your culture, your community, your school, your socioeconomic class, your religious and political affiliation, your geographic place, plus clubs, organizations, associations, and so on that you align with.*	*Describe how you see yourself as a writer, including your writing influences, your good and bad experiences with writing, your memories of writing, writing habits, writing passion, and writing skills.*

And on and on it goes. The maps often launch memories or stories that will inform students' philosophy of writing. I also invite students to write a literacy narrative using a mentor text.

Writing About Writing Using Sentence Stems

Writing about writing is something a lot of writers do. (For a great resource of writers writing about writing, check out the *New York Times* Writers on Writing archive.) In *The Modern Library Writer's Workshop*, Stephen Koch (2003) says, "In interviews and letters, in table talk and memoirs and manifestos, writers have always held forth in surprisingly full detail about how they do what they do" (xiv). Over time, if students write about writing as a writer, if they analyze their own writing as a professional writer would, they begin to identify with their own process. Legitimacy forms. Authenticity emerges. Helping kids see themselves as writers by writing about their own writing deeply changes their outlook on the practice.

You could compare this kind of analysis with what professional athletes do when they watch game or practice footage to improve their skill. Analyzing footage is the pro-football equivalent of students reflecting on what they know about writing. The only difference is pro athletes watch and analyze their performance visually, and writers analyze their writing through writing. By using the same medium to probe the very skill they're analyzing, they reap the rewards of practice, reflection, and analysis. This habit also reinforces the notion that students are writers because they are writing and reflecting on their own process like professional writers.

I ask students to select a single piece of writing they did the previous year and write a play-by-play of the process of the piece. This is really hard to do, but it's an assignment that sheds a lot of light on their process and the attitudes and beliefs they hold about writing. After this activity, Erica wrote in her notebook, "Even though I enjoyed writing, I would often not finish my writing because I never thought it was good enough. I used to tell myself that I did not care what people thought, to keep me away from my emotions."

Another way I ask students to start thinking about their own writing is through the simple, yet effective tool of sentence stems. Sentence stems create a writing invitation that even the most reluctant writer can step into, writing from their personal life to declare a truth.

Here's a general script for this invitation: Open your writing notebook. In five minutes, generate as many sentences that begin with "Writing is . . ." or "A writer is . . ." as you can. If you want to write a bulleted list, that's fine. If you want to write in sentences or paragraphs, that's fine too. Complete the sentences as many times as you want with new information even if that information may be contradictory to another statement you've made earlier.

Sarah loves country music and wearing camo. She's always reading some serial killer slasher novel. She's a math whiz and a drummer in our school's marching band, taking her role very seriously by dedicating hours and hours of practice time on the field.

Sarah writes:

> A writer is anyone who is brave enough to share every layer of themselves. Whether it be through stories, poems, screenplays, a simple sentence. A writer is anyone who can take their worst days and make someone else's day better. A writer is anyone who believes in the power of words and how they're constructed. A writer is anyone whose loneliness can be comforted by the keyboard, pencil, paper, etc. A writer's anyone who can have a deep conversation with just themselves.

From this excerpt, I see that Sarah is devoted to writing as an emotive mode of expression, one where self-discovery and truth are at the center. I can use Sarah's philosophy of writing as a cornerstone on which to build skills she may lack. Knowing she believes writing is a form of therapy is a great window into her process and possible future topics, forms, or modes I can suggest she pursue.

For example, I suggested the form of the open letter to Sarah, knowing that she believes being a writer is someone having "a deep conversation with just themselves." The open letter form was a mode she found useful to express both her excitement and sadness about graduating high school and moving on to the next stage in her life.

Another student, Promise, approached the stem differently, creating more of a poetic answer. Promise's father is a minister from the Ivory Coast who came to Lexington to work with a church community. She and her siblings speak French at home, English at school, and she's also fluent in Spanish. Her faith and her family are central to her life, and she loves math and science, but she is also a poet, someone for whom writing is an escape and a means of tempering the slights of the world.

Promise writes:

A writer is someone who can write better than they talk

A writer is a person who can sense the world around them in a different kind of way

A writer is someone that observes and listens

A writer is an eavesdropper

A writer is uncensored and cannot be kept from telling the truth

They are truth tellers

Writers are creative, imagistic beings

Writers are skilled in keeping secrets

Writers are creators, world builders

Writers are undefined, yet love to define

Writers are people who perceive things and situations in different manners

Promise's declarations are as much about her philosophy of writing as they are about who she is as a writer. Her imagination, her fluency with words are all on display here as well as many insights into her craft. Reading this early in the semester gave me a great deal of awareness of Promise's writing self-concept, how she sees the work of writing, and the special place she holds in her life for the craft.

Next steps for sentence stems: Rewrite one of your new sentences at the top of a clean page, then write the *story* or *stories* from your life that taught you that this sentence is true. What is the reason you believe this statement to be true? What proof or evidence from your life has made you believe this statement is true? Share with a partner and discuss what sentence you chose and the story that taught you this.

Writing a Philosophy of Writing

To be as open with my students as I can about writing, I share with them my writing philosophy or a bunch of thoughts I have about writing. I write these each year; sometimes I have four points, sometimes six, but the core sentiments remain the same. I also ask students to write their own philosophy at the beginning of the year and then again at the end of the year. They compare them to see if their beliefs around the act of writing have changed in nine months.

Sharing these truths with my students helps me ease them into discovering their own writing philosophy. Plus it generates a lot of good classroom conversation. I typically write the following four belief statements on the board and ask students to silently assign them as true or false. Then we discuss and unpack them. Here are this year's statements.

Writing is a performance skill.

Writing is often taught as a series of rules students need to learn or formulas they need to memorize to later execute. But this portrays writing as a canon of laws instead of the fluid performative act that it is. It would be foolish, for example, to prevent soccer players from practicing toe touches or sole rolls unless they had first memorized and tested proficiently on a soccer rulebook. Of course, rules are necessary to make the game of soccer watchable and playable, and players need to know the rules to play well, but the rules never substitute for the actual moves and thrill of the game or the practice that makes the game possible. Making writing about the rules that govern communication instead of the communication itself overlooks the most exhilarating part of writing—the discovery, the creation, and the expression of thought.

Writing requires practice, practice, practice.

When students are required to write one single essay at the end of a unit instead of writing dozens of different pieces throughout the year, they don't get the kind of practice that leads to proficiency. In *Art and Fear: Observations on the Perils (and Rewards) of Artmaking*, writers David Bayles and Ted Orland (1993) tell a story about a ceramics teacher who split his pottery class into two groups on the first day of class. One group would be graded on making the best pot they could and the second group would be graded on how many pots they made. The study revealed that the students who made lots of pots knew more about the art of pottery and typically had made better pots than the students who worked on one the entire term. When students experience the "championship game" form of writing instruction, they work and rework the same single piece of writing, like replaying the same game over and over in an effort to achieve flawlessness instead of playing many games to achieve growth.

Writing is complex.

Here's a paradox. The mysterious, dizzy chaos of life coexists with a brain that seeks order and logic by which to make sense of the chaotic and the mysterious. This inter-section is where writing is born. Writing requires knowing something, yet not fully understanding it or not being able to express it, and being OK with that. You have something to say while simultaneously recognizing you will never say it as well as you'd like. The confounding process of writing is both creative and dogmatic. Writing is both the process by which you produce work and the work itself.

What are you doing? *Writing*.

What will you have when you're done? *Writing*.

Writing, then, is a complex and personal process that relies on more than a dozen cognitive, kinesthetic, visual, verbal, and logical functions, acting both singularly and simultaneously in multiple and recursive ways. Writing also depends on rules that govern language, foundational principles about how words, sentences, and paragraphs represent images and ideas. This too is a paradox.

A personal aside: traditional public education doesn't do well with the nuanced, the paradoxical, or the complex. We like our content measurable, preferably in tidy forty-five-minute testable lessons. And because of that, when we come up against a personal process like writing, so complex and unique, yet one that also acts within certain guidelines, we glom onto the rules at the expense of the complex.

Writing requires failure.

In most American classrooms, we still proceed as if failure is a bad thing. And yet, failing as a writer is the only way you learn how to write. Elite bodybuilders might call this "training to failure," doing as many reps as possible with good form until you can't possibly lift another ounce. This practice increases strength and muscular endurance by breaking down the muscle to make it stronger. Writing is the same; we lift and push and pump a paragraph until we can't possibly revise it with any other variation. We fail and learn, flop and sweat, always becoming smarter about our process.

Of course, none of this feels good. In fact, in any other area of my life—my finances, my marriage, my health—failure may be catastrophic, and I want to avoid it. But when I hit the gym to lift or when I arrive at my writing desk, I have to steel myself with this knowledge: lifting to failure makes it possible for me to make the small gains that will increase my strength, and failing to write exactly the idea as it gloriously appeared in my head makes it possible for me to revise the emergent into something better.

> To ask students to write their own philosophy of writing, you could use the sentence stems from the previous activity as a starter or ask them to write four sentences with "Writing is . . ." or "Writing requires . . ." as four subheadings. To tap into students' core beliefs, I urge them to write only single sentences they believe to be absolutely true. After writing that single sentence, they tell the one story or a combination of stories from their own life that has taught them the truth of this statement.

As a teacher of writing, you have multiple experiences around the art of teaching, but you also hold beliefs about the craft of writing as well. These beliefs may have been formed in high school or college or last week in your writing group. The point is, you have a philosophy that dictates how you approach both writing and the teaching of writing. To ask your students to examine their own philosophy of writing would be premature before unpacking your own.

Make a weekend date with yourself and stake out your own writing philosophy. Parse it down to a few sentences you believe are true and defensible about the act of writing. Write the story of why you believe these maxims to be true. Leave them alone for a few weeks to a month. Return to them and see how they hold up. At some point in the year, share your list with your students. Ask them to put *true* or *false* next to each of your statements to see what they think about your truth. Then ask your students to write their own. Share and discuss.

Comparing Drafts to Published Work

One of the hallmarks of writing identity is walking away from writing that isn't working, knowing what to cut out and what to leave in. Knowing how to revise builds resiliency and autonomy in student writers. However, when I give students mentor texts, the revision decisions the writer made are largely hidden. Mentor texts are the result of hundreds of hours of take-outs-and-put-ins resulting in the sealed-in-resin smoothness of the finished piece.

Showing students not just a mentor text, but also some examples of the first stumbling drafts of that text is critical. This activity helps to dismantle the myth that writers know exactly what they want to say before they begin to write. This summer, I discovered a delightful example in the *New York Times*' series Close Read. Dwight Garner and Parul Sehgal (2021) analyze Elizabeth Bishop's famous villanelle "One Art," using pictures of Bishop's drafts to show her process. The analysis tracks Bishop's decisions from the "prose-heavy first draft" with "several possible titles." This early draft features references to Bishop's partner Alice Methfessel, whom she was separated from when she wrote the poem. In the first drafts, there is clear evidence of Methfessel. Bishop writes about "an 'average-sized' person with 'blue eyes' and 'fine hands.'"

And yet, Garner and Sehgal (2021) write, "Over more than a dozen drafts, we can see how Bishop transmuted the personal into something larger. As she revises, Methfessel's presence flickers." By draft 11, only her partner's "aster" eyes survive the cut. And in the final version of the villanelle, Bishop drops any mention of the eyes at all.

These drafts are fantastic examples of how writing comes to be. Showing students the progression of a poem with evidence of the poet's aims growing and transforming is a great lesson in the kind of decisions they need to feel comfortable making. An outstanding lesson in revision, these drafts showcase a writing identity in action.

In 1958, Hemingway admitted to George Plimpton and the readers of *The Paris Review* that he had rewritten the ending of *Farewell to Arms* more than three dozen times before he was satisfied. In 2012, Scribner issued a Hemingway Library Edition of the novel that included all the endings, along with drafts of other passages. As an object lesson, I print out several of these alternate endings and ask my students to observe and discuss the similarities and differences. Pairing any final draft with previous drafts serves as a great way to examine a writer's literacy craft and artistic choices.

Similarly, E. B. White revised a 1969 *New Yorker* piece on the historic moon landing numerous times. To teach close reading and the importance of revision, I use copies of drafts 3 and drafts 6 of this paragraph (found on the Harvard College Writing Program's Writing Center [Saltz 1998]) to also teach students the power of bold writerly decisions. Showing students these versions leads to conversations about choice and decision making. For the student of writing, these images are incredibly informative. The revision never ends.

I also show them working drafts of a three hundred–word blog post I have revised three times: each permutation is closer, leaner, sharper in focus. They can track the changes easily. Discussions ensue. Students ask: How do I know when a piece is finished? How do I know when to zig and when to zag? How do writers do it? If we were to have an audience with Bishop, Hemingway, and White, they may not know the answer to any of these questions either. But they're important ones to ask. And even more important than asking these questions is the raising of awareness for students about the moveable feast of writing and how writing identity is the main ingredient of all good revision.

Teaching Writing Is Hard

Unpack Your Own Writing Identity

I've been a writer for nearly four decades. And yet, no matter how many articles, books, blogs, or essays I've written, every time I sit down to write, somewhere in the back of my mind, a voice says: *The jig is up. You may have written before, but* now *you have nothing to say. You did passably well at those other ventures, but the well has run dry.*

In these moments, everything sounds wrong. If my ideas aren't trite, they are muddled; if my language isn't wooden, it's purple, and my sentences, windbaggy. How do I get what's in my head out on paper? Everything comes out at once or not at all. I don't write in chronological order or in any order at all. I often don't know where to start or where to end. The choices are overwhelming. Arranging, cutting, organizing the work so that a single point comes into view takes time and a concentrating space.

Of course, the best path is to plunge right in, but even ginning up the courage to plunge is also work. The pledge to meet myself daily on the page is a gamble that I will feel better for having done it, but not a guarantee. Although it

becomes easier over time and with success, this diligence requires weekly tend-
ing, which is both exhilarating and tedious. I'm also burdened by the fear of
being exposed as a hack, an imposter. The critical voice in my head says, *Just
who do you think you are?*

Yet because I am a writer, I anticipate these voices. I know they're going to
show up. I know they're false. And I know that the act of writing overcomes
them. Being a writer necessitates I write consistently to overcome the resistance
that *not* writing will produce. Forging past their hectoring voices somehow vali-
dates my identity as a writer by doing the very thing that gives me the most
anxiety.

Writing is no less stressful, less taxing, less arduous for my students, who
may not have had any success as a writer. Or any less stressful for the English
teacher who is attempting to teach writing to less-than-thrilled students and
whose last sustained writing task may have been her master's thesis seventeen
years ago. Perhaps writing is even more stressful for her because she's standing
in front of a group of students attempting to lead them in an activity that she
herself is anxious about.

Although teachers may have had several undergraduate or graduate classes
on teaching reading, many may have never had a single class on teaching writing
and may feel underprepared to lead students in the practice. Teaching content,
like math, doesn't require becoming a mathematician, although that certainly
helps, but teaching a skill, like fishing or biking or writing, requires you are a
practitioner or have been a practitioner of the endeavor in which you hope to
lead others. Most English teachers identify as readers because they read and love
to read, but they feel like a fraud when asked if they are writers. For the ten years
I served as codirector of the Morehead Writing Project, I watched this struggle
play out during our invitational institute. Teachers from all content areas and all
grade levels would show up that first day nervous about committing four weeks
of their summer to the act of writing, apprehensive about their ability to stay the
course, and hesitant to introduce themselves as "Hi, my name is . . . , and I'm a
writer."

Maybe they had defined a writer only as a published author or they may not
have written regularly, but just as our students who were writing for nearly 88
percent of their classes but not identifying as writers, teachers, many of whom
write daily for their job, didn't see themselves that way either.

The foundational philosophy of the National Writing Project is that the best writing teacher is a teacher who writes, and our summers were spent discovering the wisdom of that maxim. For the ten years I served as codirector, 75 to 80 percent of our teachers each summer formed a writing identity during the four weeks we were together. Helping teachers form a writing identity was our main goal because this identity would benefit the teachers the most when they returned to their classrooms in the fall. Possessing a writing identity would help them make solid instructional decisions, for example, when an administrator or curriculum coach suggested that they teach writing with the latest silver bullet. By shoring up their identity as writers, they gained credibility as a teacher and writer and understood more fully how to assist that discovery and exploration in their students.

Why Being a Teacher Who Writes Is ~~Necessary~~ Helpful

So much of what passes for instructional sorcery imposed on teachers by their districts or departments could be stopped with two questions: Does learning happen like this in the real world? Do readers and writers do this in the real world? Unfortunately, learning in school and learning in the real world often don't look alike. Did anyone ever learn how to be a writer from correcting ten of someone else's disembodied sentences? No. I don't even have to search the literature for that answer.

And that's reason enough for you to become a writer. You can just say no to newfangled writing gospels. You can protect your students from bad practice. You can use your own experience as a resource. You can conference with students from a place of co-joy and co-misery, not in a hierarchy where you have to consult a key for the answers. You can model your writing practice and reflect on your own experience. Your identity as a writer strengthens your identity as a teacher and vice versa.

Developing a writing practice is an ongoing journey of professional bravery that is free, always available, and 100 percent tailored for you. You will deepen your knowledge of craft and your understanding of revision, structure, and organization.

Confronting and naming one's own struggles with writing is as imperative to the teaching of writing as being a writer is. Examining one's own reservations creates an awareness of what you might be unconsciously telepathing to your students. The paradox is this: exposing my limitations in the content I teach doesn't negate my authority; it enhances it. It's one thing for me to write books and maybe share a chapter draft with my students, but it's an entirely different thing to hand out a short story in progress and tell them I'm in the weeds because I can't find my groove, and I'm feeling despair. But what a great lesson that is for them. And what a great lesson in vulnerability for me.

When students come to you and explain they don't know how to get started on a writing task, what is your answer? As a writer, you can tell them your story. Of a writing task that stymied you, of the procrastination and perfectionism you battle, of how you worked through it, of how you're still working through it. This, the sharing of your story, is the most effective lesson you can deliver, but it requires a practice, time and attention.

Time is our enemy. As teachers, we have so little of it. And writing requires trial and error. Which is timely. Writing is also about truth telling and meaning making, a timely exercise that comes with an emotional and cognitive cost as well. Self-concept is another enemy. Perhaps proclaiming yourself as a writer feels pretentious unless you've achieved some level of accomplishment. Fair enough. But can you imagine any other skill wherein the teachers didn't practice the skill they were imparting to their students? A trucker who didn't truck? A fisher who didn't fish?

In the face of the frantic, daily grind of being a full-time teacher, I find there are a few things that make time slow down. One of them is walking in nature, another is meditating, and the one I enjoy the most is writing. All three exercises require me to slow down and pay attention—when I'm walking, I'm paying attention to the path, the trees, and the nature around me. When I'm meditating, I'm thinking about my breath—in and out, in and out. And when I'm writing, I'm thinking about connecting experience to language to keystrokes. All three activities produce a stillness in me that makes time deepen and hollow out the tense places in my shoulders and back. If you are a harried teacher (and by that I mean, if you are a teacher), do yourself a favor. Make time to make time slow down with writing.

How do you feel about yourself as a writer? Where would you rank your writerly self-regard on a scale from 1 to 5, with 1 being "I am not a writer" to 5 being "I am a writer"? Why do you rank yourself this way? What experiences have formed this core belief about yourself?

3-1

Who were your writing mentors? Teachers, writers, friends, writing community peers? What experiences shaped your life as a writer?

3-2

How would you describe your writing process to your students? How would you characterize your writing skill? What strategies have you used to overcome writing resistance? What are your writing preferences? What are your writing habits?

3-3

Select a writing assignment you often give your students during the course of the year. Perhaps it's a personal narrative, a sonnet, or an analytical essay. Imagine yourself as a student in your classroom. You've read the material, looked over the rubric, done the research. How do you proceed? Describe the process you would take if you were asked to write this piece of writing. Does it match with the process that most of your students take in writing? What is alike or different about your approach?

3-4

Select a writing assignment you often give your students during the course of the year and write a model for your students. Save all the drafts, including any notes you take, research, zero drafts, feedback from peers, and so on. Find a space in your room where you can set up a minimuseum with all these archives of your process for students to walk through and make observations about how you process writing.

3-5

Committing to Time

One of the most essential gifts writing teachers can give themselves is time to write. But with our thirty-six-hour obligations, how do we find it? Julia Cameron (1992) in *The Artist's Way* suggests writing three pages every morning as soon as you get out of bed. But if you have children to wrangle and buses to catch, this is impossible. I've always wanted to be one of those writers who could rise at 4:00 a.m. and write for two hours before going to work. I did this in fact for one semester, and it was an unmitigated disaster. I'm just not built for that schedule.

Other teachers write when their students write, which is also a great practice. Many of my colleagues consider the writing time they spend with their students the most valuable classroom time of all. They can be transparent about their process in clear and present ways as they write. I've never been able to do this consistently. When I'm in my writing head, I'm not in the classroom; I'm not even in the same universe. It's dangerous to leave a classroom of even the most compliant teens alone for long stretches of time while I sit in a trance in the corner.

Other teachers write in short bursts, snatching fifteen minutes of writing time when they can amid the hurry-scurry. This is my habit. As a classroom teacher, I can't adhere to an extended writing practice. But I can do what most writers whose day jobs consumed their time have done throughout history: write in the cracks and crannies of my day.

I realized I worked better when I wrote for fifteen minutes at my school desk before I started my day. Before I checked my email or headed to the copy room, I opened a Google Doc and wrote. I might also write fifteen minutes or so in my journal before going to bed—just processing the day or ranting about something or trying to count my blessings and be grateful. I was more committed to writing in these moments when I had a goal or a product in mind: a blog I wanted to post, a chapter I wanted to deliver, a short story with a deadline. Going through my day, the off-task part of my mind was mulling and playing with ideas.

I also wrote in faculty meetings, during church, in doctor's offices. I wrote briefly in the cracks of time I carved out, then wrote longer during weekends, holiday breaks, and the summer. My crack writing wasn't pretty or profound. But like all daily commitments, it was the showing up that counted. I wrote in Google Keep, or my iPhone notes, or the Evernote app. Sometimes I recorded ideas with the Voice Record Pro app during my commute and then transcribed them when I got to school. This practice built my writing fluency, helped me keep in touch with my writing self, provided me dozens of seed ideas, and helped me process my world. Limiting myself to ten or fifteen minutes made that time precious, but it helped me to ignore the critical voice of perfection in my head and get something down.

Of course, the kind of writing I'm suggesting here is not big, publishable, outside writing; it's inside writing, personal and messy. But this inside practice makes taking one's ideas outside possible. As *New York Times* columnist and literary theorist Stanley Fish (2011) says, "It may sound paradoxical, but verbal fluency is the product of hours spent writing about nothing" (26). This kind of writing produces ideas and snippets, which can be parlayed into finished, publishable pieces, if you should desire.

Adding one more thing to your to-do list is a challenge, but for me, writing is an antidote to modern madness, a calm in the insistent ping of Breaking News or That Very Important Thing, all ringing for my attention. Even though it is a struggle, writing brings me into the present moment, restoring and refreshing me in the way a good nap or quick jog does.

Maybe writing doesn't do that for you. Maybe there's great foreboding that someone might read what you've written. Maybe even scribbles in a private notebook come loaded with an internal voice of censure. That's OK. That's what this chapter aims to unpack. Just trust that the practice of writing is valuable to your identity as a writer and a teacher and that showing up on the page daily is a commitment you will not regret.

Committing to Vulnerability

"I'm not self-actualized on all these myself," said Dr. Caryn Huber, my dean of students, to a faculty of two hundred teachers during our opening day. She was introducing a PowerPoint that featured behaviors we'd like our students to develop for academic and emotional success.

It was a surprising admission. I wrote it down. It's the first time I'd ever heard an administrator or anyone leading a professional development say this out loud: that every day we ask kids to act in ways we adults haven't mastered yet.

We ask kids to set SMART (specific, measurable, achievable, relevant, and time-bound) goals, manage their time well, bounce back in the face of failure, interact with peers not of their social group, be compassionate, be responsive, be engaged, be curious, be driven, and be goal-oriented. But the truth of the adult world is very few of us have that list in the bag.

Does anyone have their ego in check? How many of us respond with compassion every single time? How many of us sit with new people at faculty meetings? Judge not? Give more than we receive?

Dr. Huber's admission was a rarity. Admitting our humanness isn't on center stage at most professional development events. Yet the foundation of our most powerful selves is our humanity, our mistakes, our weak spots. If our own struggle to learn is not on display in our classrooms, it's a waste of a powerful demonstration of what it means to be a real learner and a real human.

I'm describing a commitment to vulnerability. I'm a fan of shame researcher Dr. Brene Brown (2012), whose work on vulnerability has exploded in the last ten years. She identifies vulnerability as "the catalyst for courage, compassion, and connection" (11), a trifecta of virtues teachers need. And yet, in her research, she discovered 85 percent of the people she interviewed remembered an incident during school as being so profoundly shaming it changed the way they learned; she calls this "creativity scars" (198), a specific memory of being told as a child that you weren't a good singer or artist or dancer or writer.

I had dinner with a colleague recently who told me about failing her Google certification test, and the empathy she developed for those students who try and try to learn content they just can't master. She shared her failure with her students; in fact, she wrote a blog post about it and gave it to them to read. I'm suggesting there's no difference in your students' journey and your own. Sharing your own hills and valleys makes their path less scary. We often present ourselves at guru status when revealing our own challenges would be more instructive. And by instructive, I mean it teaches *us*, not necessarily our students. It helps *us* develop compassion and identify with their struggles.

When I was a young teacher, Kentucky students were required to submit six pieces of their writing in a portfolio to be scored by the state. I noticed that students in classrooms where teachers drearily presented this work as "We are writing *for* the portfolio" were much less enthused and less engaged than those students whose teachers framed the work as "We have a portfolio because we are *writers*." Of course, there are host of variables that impact student engagement, but a teacher's attitude is near the top. If you were writing shamed by some crone in middle school, do you carry that insecurity decades later as you attempt to teach this skill around which you have no confidence? Many of us carry our own scars into the classroom, projecting our own unexamined wounds onto our students through cynicism, perfectionism, or shaming. Becoming mindful of our own education opens up a valuable avenue of healing.

Committing to a Writing Practice

When you commit to writing, you also commit to time and vulnerability because you can't have one without the other two. Writing takes time and creates self-discovery in a way that dismantles the ego. Writing with your students will create vulnerability too, breaking down the student–teacher relationship in a way that creates powerful community. But this investment, like all things of value, is worth it. Cultivating a personal writing practice has made me a better writing teacher, but it does come at a cost.

Maybe you already have a committed writing practice. Throughout this chapter, I invite you to write, to think about your own writing history, your misgivings, joys, and frustrations with writing, so you can share, listen, learn, and give back to the writers in your classrooms.

Writing identity is a social, emotional, and cognitive construct. It's something you may possess, but not be able to readily define. Something you may glimpse from time to time, but not truly grasp. As such, it's instructive at this point to unpack your writing history, examine your writing experiences, and identify the characteristics of your own attitudes and beliefs around writing.

Unpacking Your Writing History

As we enter school, we have both positive and negative writing experiences and form attitudes around the act of writing. To unearth and track your awareness of yourself as a writer is to understand yourself better as a writing teacher. For example, if you were shamed as a middle school student for sentence fragments or grammar issues, you might be either hypervigilant or hyperpassive about teaching syntax and usage to your students.

You can use the following prompts with your students or find a space where you can be alone and undisturbed for ten minutes, maybe at lunch or on the subway or on a Saturday morning before the kids wake up. Turn off all distractions. Into this space, bring only your choice of writing implements—notebook and pen, laptop, iPad, whatever. Get comfortable. Take a deep breath, then look over the following prompts. Pick one or two. Without thinking too much, just write it down on the top of your page. Write a certain amount of time (five minutes is a good start) or write a certain about of writing (one handwritten page is a good start). Don't censor yourself. No one will read this but you. Just whatever pops into your head is probably the truest response.

3-6
Think back over your formative writing life and tell the story of how you learned to write. What is an early memory of writing before you were in school? Did you observe your parents or older siblings writing? How did that impact your awareness of writing? Who taught you to write your name? Did you write letters before you entered school? Who taught you? Do you remember tracing letters? Did someone other than a teacher teach you to hold a pencil and write? What implements did you use to write?

3-7
Think about the writing you did during your time in elementary school. What are one or two memories you have of writing in elementary school? Do you still have the writing? What were some of the writing assignments you remember from that time in your life? Were your experiences with writing mostly positive or mostly negative?

3-8
Think about the writing you did during your middle or high school years. What are one or two memories you have of writing in middle or high school? Do you still have the writing? What were some of the writing assignments you remember from that time in your life? Were your experiences with writing mostly positive or mostly negative?

3-9
Think about the writing you did during your undergraduate, graduate, or doctoral experience. What are one or two memories of writing during these years? Did you embrace or resist the rigors of academic discourse required in college classes? Did you take a class in creative writing, science writing, nature writing, or another kind of writing, such as playwriting, poetry, or screenwriting? Did you ever visit the university writing center or receive tutoring in writing? Do you still have copies of your writing from this time in your life?

3-10
Think about the writing you do on the job. What are one or two memories you have of writing an extended piece of writing (beyond short emails) that required planning and revision? Do you write models of essays for your

students? Are you required to write a reflection as part of your personal growth plan? Do you regularly write with a group of peers? Do you regularly write and share with your students? What kind of professional writing have you done over the past five years?

Leave the writing you did from the previous prompts for a day or two and then look back over them. Do you see patterns emerge? Do you see any resistance or a theme of shame surrounding the act of writing? Or do you see an eagerness, a rushing toward the act, a desire to write more? Do vestiges from your writing history show up in your writing instruction as positivity or negativity? Reviewing your history as a writer will reveal many of the attitudes, values, and beliefs you might unconsciously hold as a writing teacher. For five minutes, write about how your attitudes toward writing or teaching writing might influence how you approach writing or the teaching of writing. Continue to analyze your findings by asking why.

Unpacking Your Writing Attitudes

One of the easiest and best tools for writing with students are simple, low-stakes writing activities using sentence stems. Even the most antiwriting students I've had in writing classes can't resist the invitation of an unfinished sentence just waiting for them to fill in their own hot take (see Figure 3–1).

In writing, as with meditating, the goal is just to stay on the page. Tibetan Buddhist nun Pema Chodron's (1997) advice to those who wish to meditate is to sit with the discomfort it may produce. "Give yourself instructions like you would a dog: stay, stay, stay" (26). The goal is not comfort; it's learning to sit with discomfort. This is good advice for writers. Keep writing. Stay with it. Be vulnerable. That's the goal.

Another way to examine our biases around the act of writing is to examine our attitudes. These two surveys, a Writing Attitude Survey (Figure 3–2) and a Teaching Writing Attitude Survey (Figure 3–3), are adapted from Larry Podson's (1997) *Written Expression* (Rafanello 2008) and are designed to collect some data about your writing attitudes regarding both writing and teaching writing.

Figure 3–1 ~ *Unpacking Your Writing Attitudes with Sentence Stems*

Following are nine sentence stems for you. Without thinking too much, finish each sentence stem. Just whatever pops into your head is probably the truest response. Don't censor yourself. Write quickly. Don't think about what each sentence says about you or how it makes you look. No one is looking over your shoulder. This is just you and your notebook, doing a little practice.

As a writer, I am . . .

As a teacher, I am . . .

As a writing teacher, I am . . .

When I write, I sometimes feel . . .

When I teach, I sometimes feel . . .

When I teach writing, I sometimes feel . . .

As a writer, I wish . . .

As a teacher, I wish . . .

As a writing teacher, I wish . . .

- After completing all the sentences, look back over your list and settle on one of them that speaks to you, the sentence that wants more sentences to be written after it.

- Rewrite that new sentence at the top of a clean page, and write after it for five minutes, telling the *story* or *stories* from your life that taught you this sentence is true.
  - » What is the reason you believe this statement to be true?
  - » What proof or evidence from your life has made you believe this statement is true?

- Write for a second five-minute session, unpacking that same sentence, but this time analyzing it or making an argument for it. There is no right or wrong way to do this. Just write.

- Look at the two entries and analyze.
  - » Do you see any patterns?
  - » Could you blend the narrative of your story into an argument or analysis?
  - » Is this piece the beginning of a personal essay?
  - » Could this piece find its way into a professional journal?

To complete the survey, circle your response, from strongly disagree to strongly agree, that indicates your feelings about the statement. Add your scores in each column, then calculate them together for your grand total. The higher the score, the more positive, more confident writing attitude.

Figure 3–2 ~ *Writing Attitude Survey*

	Strongly Disagree	Disagree	Don't Know	Agree	Strongly Agree
I avoid writing whenever possible.	5	4	3	2	1
I have no fear of my writing being evaluated.	1	2	3	4	5
I look forward to writing down my ideas.	1	2	3	4	5
I am afraid of writing when I know it might be evaluated.	5	4	3	2	1
My mind seems to go blank when I start writing.	5	4	3	2	1
Expressing my ideas through writing is a waste of time.	5	4	3	2	1
I would enjoy submitting my writing to magazines for evaluation and publication.	1	2	3	4	5
I like to write my ideas down.	1	2	3	4	5
I feel confident in my ability to express my ideas in writing.	1	2	3	4	5
I like to have my friends read what I have written.	1	2	3	4	5
I'm nervous about my writing.	5	4	3	2	1
People seem to enjoy what I write.	1	2	3	4	5
I enjoy writing.	1	2	3	4	5
I never seem to be able to write down my ideas clearly.	5	4	3	2	1
I'm not a good writer.	5	4	3	2	1
I like seeing my thoughts on paper.	1	2	3	4	5
Discussing my writing with others is an enjoyable experience.	1	2	3	4	5
Writing letters of recommendation for my students creates anxiety for me.	5	4	3	2	1
I don't think I teach writing as well as most people.	5	4	3	2	1
Writing is a lot of fun.	1	2	3	4	5
Total					
Grand total					

Circle your response, from strongly disagree to strongly agree, that indicates your feeling about the statement. Add your scores in each column, then calculate them together for your grand total. The higher the score, the more positive, more confident your attitude is toward teaching writing.

Figure 3–3 ~ *Teaching Writing Attitude Survey*

	Strongly Disagree	Disagree	Don't Know	Agree	Strongly Agree
I avoid teaching writing if possible.	5	4	3	2	1
I have no fear of my writing instruction being evaluated.	1	2	3	4	5
I look forward to teaching students how to write.	1	2	3	4	5
I am afraid to teach a writing lesson when I'm being observed by a peer or my administrator.	5	4	3	2	1
I don't know the best way to teach writing.	5	4	3	2	1
Teaching students to write is a waste of time.	5	4	3	2	1
I enjoy giving feedback on student writing.	1	2	3	4	5
I like to teach all aspects of writing.	1	2	3	4	5
I feel confident in my ability to teach writing.	1	2	3	4	5
I like it when my colleagues ask me to help them plan writing instruction.	1	2	3	4	5
I'm nervous about teaching writing.	5	4	3	2	1
Students tell me I make writing easy to understand.	1	2	3	4	5
I enjoy teaching writing.	1	2	3	4	5
I never know the best way to plan a writing lesson.	5	4	3	2	1
I'm not a good writing teacher.	5	4	3	2	1
I like watching a video of myself teaching writing.	1	2	3	4	5
Discussing my writing instruction with others is an enjoyable experience.	1	2	3	4	5
Writing models to share with my students creates anxiety for me.	5	4	3	2	1
I don't think I teach writing as well as most people.	5	4	3	2	1
Teaching writing is a lot of fun.	1	2	3	4	5
Total					
Grand total					

Take a few minutes to consider the results of the survey. Were you surprised or alarmed? Did the scores match how you feel as a writer and a writing teacher? What did this survey reveal to you? Write for a set time (five to seven minutes) or for a set number of pages (one to two pages) about one or two things the survey revealed to you about your attitudes. How might your attitudes toward writing or teaching writing influence how you approach writing or the teaching of writing?

Unpacking Your Writing Identity

As we discussed in Chapter 1, writing identity is an overlay of self-identity, social identity, and writerly self-regard, which connects both to how you see yourself as a writer and to the act of writing.

During a recent professional development in our district, I asked teachers to write and share a little about how their self-identity and social identity had strengthened or defeated their writerly self-regard. (I've also used this handout Figure 3–4 in my classroom with students.)

Stephanie, a veteran teacher of twenty-three years and ABD (All but dissertation) in Educational Leadership, wrote, "I have grown to resent research-based writing, which I used to enjoy because I was good at it. Not feeling 'good' at it has absolutely influenced my perception of myself as a writer. I see writing as a chore now, not something from which I derive pleasure or satisfaction."

Jordan, a twenty-six-year-old paraprofessional who works at my school, who has a popular Instagram poetry profile and just recently published a book of poetry, wrote, "I'm a college dropout from a kinesiology major and have never had any writing course more advanced than basic high school and college English. I have a lot to learn, and I am an infant in terms of a writer. But I don't see age as a factor in how well you write poetry, more so how long you've been writing it."

Another teacher, Henry, raised as a white evangelical in the South, wrote, "My race represents my experience and my privilege. When writing, I am always aware of the privilege that comes with my race and . . . aware of biases in my writing."

Figure 3–4 ∼ *How Does Self-Identity and Social Identity Influence My Writing?*

When you pick up a pen or open a Google Doc to write, your sense of both self-identity and social identity comes with you. How do these identities inform or influence what, how, and whom you write about?

Directions:

In the following cells, answer these questions:

- How does this element of your identity impact your writing?
- How does this element influence the topics you choose or the way you write?
- How does this element impact the audiences for which you write?

There are no right or wrong answers. You can write as much or as little as you would like. You can jot down bullet points or write in paragraph form.

Your Age	
Your Values	
Your Personality	
Your Grade Level	
Your Race or Ethnicity	
Your Nationality	
Your Gender	
Your Socioeconomic Status	
Your Religion or Belief System	

These three responses exemplify the wide range of self-identities and social histories and experiences teachers bring to their own craft. If these three professionals were students in my class, how dramatically differently they might approach a writing task and the teaching of writing as well.

> In what way does your self-identity impact what you write about or the audiences for which you write? In what way does your socioeconomic status, race/ethnicity, gender, sexual orientation, and family of origin impact what you write about or the audiences for which you write?

3-11

> How has other people's perception of your socioeconomic status, race/ethnicity, gender, or sexual orientation impacted what you write about? How you write? The audiences for which you write? The subjects you write about?

3-12

> How has being part of a specific social, political, or cultural community impacted what you write about? How you write? The audiences for which you write? The subjects you write about?

3-13

> Fiction writer Alice McDermott writes: "I write about Catholics because I am one, a cradle Catholic, and so I know the language and the detail. This saves me from having to do too much research. Because I am a Catholic, the language of ritual, its repetitions and refrains, appeals to me and so finds its way into my work" (2021, 170). What aspect of your identity is so instinctual and innate that you know "the language and the detail" of it? What part of your identity is so ingrained into who you are that you wouldn't have to research to write about it? How does the language and the detail of this identity find its way into your writing?

3-14

Starting a Writing Practice

Starting a practice of writing is like starting any practice that requires repetition: the more habitual the practice becomes, the more fulfilling and productive the results. Whether you want to stop a destructive habit like smoking or biting your nails or start a positive habit like walking or meditating, committing to a daily practice creates momentum that will make the practice easier in the future. Here are a few tips to start:

Thirty Days to a Writing Habit

- Commit to thirty days. In a 2009 study on habit formation, researcher Phillipa Lally and her team discovered it takes, on average, about two months to change a behavior, and "it took anywhere from 18 days to 254 days for people to form a new habit" (Clear 2019). Thirty days is a good period to start with.

- Start small. To help them combat procrastination, I intentionally teach my students the five-minute rule: set a timer for five minutes and tell yourself you can quit after five minutes. But the practice is a good toe dip into a habitual writing practice as well. Try writing every day for five minutes only, either at the beginning or the end of your school day.

- Choose a writing journal. What do you like to write in? Digital document or old-school pen and paper? Choose the journal that creates the least hassle. Sometimes logging on to your MacBook and opening a file is as easy as flopping open a spiral-bound notebook. Whatever is the easiest and most accessible for you, use that.

- Choose a dedicated time. Look over your day and see where the best spots to write might occur. Right when you get out of bed? Right when you get to school? During lunch? Right after the bell rings at 3:15? While dinner is cooking? Right before you go to bed?

- Set your writing notebook somewhere in sight. Similar to packing your gym bag and leaving it by the door to increase the chances you will go to the gym, putting your writing notebook or a writing prompt list somewhere you can see it will provide the physical stimulus to remind you of your goal.

- Track a simple success metric. When an athlete trains for a goal, it is helpful to track over time a quantifiable measurement (time, distance, strength, weight, flexibility, speed, and so on) to see if gains are being made toward that goal. Businesses also track how profitable a product is performing to determine its success over time. Writers can track their record of success by printing out a simple blank calendar and marking up each day that they write. Post the calendar somewhere where you see it every day. Use stickers, a smiley face, a heart, or just a big "X" to indicate that you showed up and wrote for however many minutes you have committed to. These tracking chains create their own kind of momentum; once you have eight days in a row, it's easier to show up on the ninth day and you'll be less likely to break your commitment when you see that momentum building.

- Practice habit bundling. In *Power of Habit*, Charles Duhigg (2012) suggests habit bundling serves as a reminder to start the cue-routine-reward circuit that will build a strong practice of a behavior you want to develop (63). Bundle your first cup of coffee with five minutes of writing, then give yourself a reward at the end. (Note: This can sometimes backfire when used with students, such as when prizes are given for reading or writing. Sometimes this trains students to complete the goal for the reward, instead of achieving for the intrinsic rewards of writing and the writing process.)

- Choose a perennial writing stem. Many writers can open a journal and pour out their day on the page unbidden, but other writers need a few sentence stems to prime the pump. These stems are great because they can be used over and over and deliver different and unique sentences. Here are a few:

  » Today my teaching was . . .

  » Today my students were . . .

  » Today I felt . . .

  » Today I am grateful for . . .

  » Tomorrow I want to . . .

- Track a measurable goal. Tracking your effort over time increases your capacity. When I'm freewriting, I track word count. I set the clock for five minutes and download my brain. When I'm revising, the goal isn't necessarily word count; it's staying in the seat and getting deeper and deeper into meaning. Then I track minutes/hours at the desk. Tracking can be done on a calendar or bullet journal or just by keeping a running total in your head. You might also use an app like HabitHub or Habitica that tracks habits and keeps you motivated.

- Set some publication goals for yourself: a newsletter to parents, writing a model your whole department can use, submitting an article to a regional or national publication, submitting a creative work, like a poem or vignette, to a literary journal.

Examining Writing Experiences and Building Writerly Self-Regard

I like to get to school early for all the morning gifts. The parking lot empty, the street still dark. I badge in. Everything still and quiet except for David, the night janitor, waxing the floors at the end of the hall. I wave to him and head upstairs. My room is on the third floor with three giant windows that face east. The sun might be coming up or the moon going down. I put coffee on, and kids wander in.

One morning I was having coffee with Kailie, and she told me this wonderful story about an early writing experience.

"When I was about four years old, I wrote a story on a scrap piece of paper, but I didn't know how to write yet, so it was just letters and marks, and my uncle picked it up and acted like he was reading it, but he got the story all wrong," she said. "I was so mad."

There it was: the primitive urge to communicate thwarted by lack of skill. Kailie's experience mirrors every writer since the hymn makers of Mesopotamia. There's something so intoxicating about writing and so damning by the same stroke. We arrange these little sticks on a page to communicate the ache or joy of our hearts, but we have to arrange them *just so*.

Our core belief about who we are as writers is constructed by our lived experiences. Young writers who aren't understood by their audience or who receive a bad grade on an assignment may believe they're definitively and forevermore poor at writing. Without understanding all the other possible factors—lack of skill, lack of technique, lack of goal setting, lack of time to develop ideas, unexplained expectations, poor mentoring, and so on—student writers live out this narrative as truth. Students internalize the experience as "I'm not a good writer" or "My ideas are bad" or "Knowing how to write is something you're born with" based on an unexamined writing experience.

Of course, Kailie survived her first brush with being misunderstood as a writer. And she grew as a writer, adding skill and audience awareness to her passel of tools. Her experiences with writing were mostly positive because she had a faculty with language to begin with, but what of the students who struggle not only with learning the craft of writing, but also accumulating the necessary positive experiences with the practice to develop an identity that gives them agency?

How Writing Experiences Shape Writerly Self-Regard

As a writer learns how to control a pencil and how to arrange those jots and tittles just so, their writerly self-regard enlarges and their writing identity becomes more established. By middle and high school, students can analyze their writing experiences to see how these have shaped their identity as writers.

To help them think critically about the story they tell themselves about writing, I start with a simple visualization activity. I also want to help students think critically about their worth as a writer, which may have unconsciously been damaged and internalized from their experiences. Here is the script I use with this activity:

Visualization Script for Negative Experience with Writing

Close your eyes and think of a negative experience you have had with writing. Was it a writing assignment or something you chose to do? How old were you? Where were you? In a classroom or somewhere else? Settle into the memory, using all your senses to remember. What did you hear? What could you smell or taste? Could you touch anything in your memory? What was the strongest and most negative part of the memory? Sit with the memory and reflect on it for a few moments. Examine it calmly, watching yourself in that experience. Now open your eyes and write about this memory for five minutes, including all the details that came up during the visualization.

This activity is a powerful one for most students because they focus on a time when they failed an assignment or failed to live up to someone's expectations. The number one emotion that emerges is the shame they felt around their "bad" writing. After they write about a negative experience with writing, I use a similar script to help them remember a positive one.

Visualization Script for Positive Experience with Writing
Close your eyes and think of a positive memory you have had of writing. Was it a writing assignment or something you chose to do? How old were you? Where were you? In a classroom or somewhere else? Settle into the memory, using all your senses to remember. What did you hear? What could you smell or taste? Could you touch anything in your memory? What was the strongest and most positive part of the memory? Sit with the memory and reflect on it for a few moments. Examine it calmly, watching yourself in that experience. Now open your eyes and write about this memory for five minutes, including all the details that came up during the visualization.

This activity is another potent one for students. Many of them recount writing something personal—a letter to a loved one, a poem in a creative writing class, an assignment they worked hard on. They remember the details of this success with great clarity and pride.

After completing both the positive and negative writing experience, I ask students to analyze these two experiences side by side and answer one or two of the following questions about these experiences:

• What story or stories do you tell yourself about writing or about yourself as a writer that may have its roots in the negative experience?

- What story or stories do you tell yourself about writing or about yourself as a writer that may have its roots in the positive experience?

- What is one thing you learned about yourself or about writing from the positive experience you wrote about? What is one thing you learned from the negative experience?

- When you start a writing assignment, do you unconsciously channel the positive or the negative experience? Why?

- How could you use both your positive and negative experiences to reach out to other students who might be experiencing the same thing?

Negative experiences are hard to forget and difficult to supplant because our brain remembers danger to protect us. Avoiding writing altogether feels very smart to a student who has been shamed by the activity in the past. In *It Didn't Start with You*, Mark Wolynn (2016) suggests humans keep "only those memories that support our primitive defense structure, defenses that have been with us so long, they become us" (76). But these entrenched evolutionary defenses don't mean we have to remain stuck in reliving bad experiences over and over forever. In *The Brain That Changes Itself*, psychiatrist Dr. Norman Doidge (2007) explains that the brain's neuroplasticity allows it to reinterpret memories of our past (243). By practicing new behaviors and stimulating the brain with new experiences, humans can create new neural pathways that result in less stress and less anxiety.

Students who have previously thought of themselves as "bad" or "not good" writers can change the core language they use about themselves as writers and about the act of writing to change their writing identity. By supplanting the old, damaging narratives that limit them as writers, students can develop worth and identity by creating healthy writing practices and new stories about their own process of writing.

Five Activities to Examine Writing Experiences

In the following five activities, I challenge students to write about their writing experiences to bring to the surface any residual narratives that no longer serve their growth. By delving into their writing history, students remember writing they've done for school and writing they've done outside of school. Other fertile areas of memory are private writing experiences, such as songs, diaries, letters, or journals, and public writing experiences, such as a written testimonial for church or a speech for a civic club. The goal is to demonstrate to students that they have had experiences as writers, and that they've formed beliefs about themselves from those experiences.

Inventory of Emotions

The idea behind an inventory of emotions comes from Jewell Parker Rhodes (2001), who taught a memoir workshop at Goucher College I attended. In her workshop, she invited essayists or memoirists to create a log that tracked the emotions they associated with a memory, even before they attempted to track the details of the memory itself.

I adapted this inventory to help students remember their emotional memories around writing (Figure 4–1). The emotions that bubble up in this activity are neither good nor bad. They just are. A fourth-grade assignment to write an opinion piece could be a calamity for one student and a joyous event for another. The emotions are there for us to witness and examine and honor as part of our writing history and identity.

After students create the inventory of emotions, they spend some time analyzing the kind of writing that elicited each emotion. Predictably, the gamut of emotions for writing both in and out of school ranges from fear and anxiety to pride and achievement. Interestingly, writing for social media ranked high on their list for the kinds of writing they do outside of school, generating both pain and pleasure. There is an emotional tax to writing online content as students consider their social media persona, their audience, and the accompanying visuals within the context of the medium.

- Emma wrote: "With my personal writing, I allow myself to feel/enjoy the writing. I'm not focused on the grade/formality of the work rather than allowing myself creative fulfillment. I don't write English papers for personal enjoyment. I despise essay writing, actually. I automatically don't want to write something if it has already been 'dictated' for me. I'll still write the thing I'm supposed to write, but chances are I will still hate writing it."

Figure 4–1 ~ *Inventory of Emotions Related to Writing*

Inventory of Emotions Related to Writing	
Think over memories you have of writing in school. What emotions or feelings often accompany these memories? Write down five emotions or feelings that surround memories you associate with writing for school.	Think over memories you have of writing outside of school. What emotions or feelings often accompany these memories? Write down five emotions or feelings that surround memories you associate with writing outside of school.

- Sydney had a different take on writing for school: "I'm proud of the writing I do for English class and especially History. I know what the goal is. If I get to pick my own topic, I usually pick something I enjoy."

- Holly wrote: "If I held my piece in my hands, I would not feel joy, so I should just throw it away, right? But I can't. If I don't do my work in this class, then I'll get a bad grade, which will lower my GPA which means I'll never get into college, then I'll have to work at Home Depot for the rest of my life, and I won't make any money, so I'll live in a shitty apartment. I'll never have time to go out, so I won't ever find my husband or have kids, so basically if I don't write today, I die alone."

Holly's feelings of "no joy" surrounding writing assigned in school were pervasive. Yet writing for school is an important training ground for the writing we do for the rest of our lives primarily because it is writing someone is waiting on and for which there is a deadline.

But writing for school need not be the graveyard of broken dreams that students claim it is. Instead of seeing writing in school as drudgery accompanied by shame, students can reframe these assignments as an opportunity to grow as an independent writer. By supporting students with mentor texts and a responsive writing community, teachers can assist in this reframing by divorcing writing from high-stakes assessment to see growth, not the grade, as the goal.

Gallery of Challenges

Each year, as part of a community-building exercise, I ask students to think about the different challenges they have had in the past with writing. In the wall around my room, I create a gallery of these challenges, adapted from a similar experiment conducted with graduate student writing workshops at the University of New Castle in Australia in 2005 (Cameron, Nairn, and Higgins 2009).

On each sheet of butcher paper, I write one challenge. Students are then given a pad of sticky notes. If they have an experience with one of these challenges, they tag the challenge with a sticky note. This is a powerful silent activity that shows everyone in the room that everyone in the room faces the same trials. The challenge sheets fill up quickly with many sticky notes.

The words and phrases I use (adapted from page 273 of Cameron, Nairn, and Higgins [2009]) are:

- I have self-doubt.
- I don't know how to start.
- My ideas aren't worth talking about.
- I struggle to find research.
- I struggle to find the right tone and voice.
- I don't know what to leave out and what to leave in.
- I lack writing skills.
- I lack writing confidence.
- I fear being called out.
- I fear being compared with other writers in the room.
- I feel pressure to meet other people's expectations.

Students walk around the room and see all the emotions they thought were their own private emotional acreage are actually universal. We discuss the patterns, and then I give them some sentence stems to write a list of true statements about writing based on our common experiences:

- Every writer . . .
- Writing is always . . .
- The challenges of writing are . . .
- All writers are . . .
- As a writer, I am . . .
- As a writer, I am not . . .
- After this activity, I see that . . .
- After this activity, I understand that . . .

Start the Day Off with MetaWrites

In my writing classes, we have a practice called "Start the Day Off Write" where students choose one of three prompts to write about. Each day I post one Meta Write prompt, one personal prompt (I adapt these from Michael Gonchar's [2016] *New York Times* Learning Network resource for personal and narrative writing prompts), and one fiction or poetry prompt, which might include a line of poetry or a paragraph of fiction students can use to launch into story or poetry. (I often find these in "The Time Is Now: Writing Prompts and Exercises," a monthly feature in every *Poets and Writers* magazine. You can also sign up for weekly writing prompts through their newsletter at www.pw.org/writing-prompts-exercises.) Although there are a number of these scattered throughout this book, here are some of my favorites:

- Writer Cindy O'Donnell-Allen (2012) said, "In school, writing was a closed circuit. The teacher gave an assignment, I responded, then she passed it back with a letter grade at the top of the page. I was good at school, but none of it felt like writing. Writing was what I did on my own time. I composed poetry and song lyrics in secret and hid my journal in my sock drawer when I heard footsteps in the hall." Do you identify with this quote? What is the last thing you wrote that wasn't for a school assignment? How did this piece of writing come to be? What is one thing you've always wanted to write if you weren't being graded on it?

- When poet Rajiv Mohabir's teacher challenged him to "write something that scares you," he started writing about his childhood growing up in Florida. "To be a man of color is tough. To be a queer man of color is even tougher. I felt vulnerable being both, but I also learned to be fierce, to survive like a coyote in a pack of wolves" (Gonzales 2016, 89). If you had to write something that scares you, what would you write about? What are the lessons this fear taught you?

- In Rachel Toor's (2017) *Write Your Way In*, a book about writing college admissions essays, she urges students to use something mundane or trivial in their lives to "open out into something big." She writes: "Staying small and close to your own experience is more valuable than pronouncing on the Problem in Society Today" (23). If you were to write an essay that stayed small and close to your own experience, what are three topics you would write about? Why?

- Writer Jhumpa Lahiri wrote, "Being a writer means taking the leap from listening to others to saying, 'Listen to me'" (2011). What are five topics you can talk about at length? What topics do you love to discuss with your friends? Your family? What are a few topics that you could write about expertly with little or no research?

- Think about all the places of your childhood and the stories of those places. What are three places you're familiar with that you could write about? What perspective do you have about these places now that you are older and may have some distance from them?

- Is it important that all stories have a deeper meaning? Do all stories need to have some moral, or can they just be a good creepy story or a good funny story? Why or why not?

- Writer and teacher Matthew Salesses writes, "Revision is the craft through which a writer is able to say and shape who they are and what kind of world they live in" (2021, 39). How do you craft yourself in your writing? From what kind of world do you write? What do you have to say? What are two or three things you like to write about?

Naming the People on Your Bus

When I was a high school student, I had a lot of math anxiety. If I had told my math teachers about my past negative experience with math, the acknowledgment would have helped me for no other reason than knowing my teacher was aware of my anxiety. Asking students to share their experiences with writing is beneficial because then both of you have the knowledge of this experience. Students who acknowledge their anxiety about writing to their writing teacher feel seen and heard prior to "performing" on the page. This declaration is freeing and refreshing to students who may feel isolated and insecure in their fears.

At the beginning of Patricia Schneider's (2003) book *Writing Alone and with Others*, she invites writers to participate in a visualization exercise to do just that (22). I have used this exercise every year for the last ten years, and each year, when I ask my students to reflect over the writing activities that helped them in my class, this ranks as number one.

Patricia Schneider's Bus Exercise

Imagine yourself on a wide stretch of prairie or desert. You can see all the way to the horizon, where a little road meanders along, winding, curving. It stretches from the horizon, all the way to your feet. You are standing beside the road. Far, far in the distance, you see a bus coming toward you on the road. Let it come slowly. Perhaps there are heat waves that make it waver a bit at first. Let it come closer and closer until it draws up alongside you and stops. The door opens, and people come out one by one. Each person who gets off the bus is someone who has an opinion about your writing. (Mother? Father? Sister? Brother? Sixth-grade teacher?) The loudmouths push off first. Let them off, one by one, and let each one say what is on his or her mind. Write it down. If you want, note how the person is dressed; write that down. After all the loudmouths get off, there are some quiet folk at the back of the bus. Let them off too. What they have to say may be entirely different. After you have written the speeches of the people on the bus, you may want to do a dialogue with one or more of them.

My students love this activity because it resurrects both champions and destroyers of their writing identity, voices that criticized and voices that championed their writing efforts. I like that Schneider has room on the bus for both the positive and critical voices.

Schneider's goal with this exercise is to help writers in her workshops get rid of the internal critics, but my aim is a bit more ambitious. I want students to know that I see and hear their writing history. I also want students to see all of these voices as evidence of one thing: they are writers. Nonwriters don't get criticized because they aren't bravely writing down their thoughts for the world to see.

When students complete this activity, I ask them to reframe the

Reframing Negative Writing Experiences

- Can you apply the maxim "get curious, not furious" to this experience?

- Can you interrogate the experience?

- Can you make meaning from a negative experience?

- Can you take what you can use from a negative experience and leave the rest to rot?

- Did you learn to respect your own mind?

- Did you learn to lean into your own process?

- Did you challenge yourself to be more independent?

original experience as a learning opportunity. In other words, reappraising the experience to see the positive things that have come from even negative experiences: acknowledge the loudmouths and see what opportunities arose from that learning.

Dropping a Pin on Your Identity

One day in class, I wrote on the board, "Does what a writer writes become who a writer is?" We had just finished talking about how a writer is not her writing, and when getting feedback on our writing, it's important to remove our egos from the work so we can "hear" what people are saying. After a brief discussion on this question, my students felt writers *were* often bound by some form of external definition. You think of Stephen King as a "horror writer," or Stephanie Meyers as a "vampire writer."

This conversation may be beyond the needs of most students, but my students did recognize that typecasting limited writers. Writers who declare "I am a poet" or "I write sci-fi" or "I am a blogger" become attached to the form of writing as their identity instead of their writing practice. Possessing a writing identity, knowing your way around a piece of writing, they decided, was better than labeling themselves a poet or a blogger or screenwriter.

If writing identity is only tied to what someone has written instead of someone's practice of writing, writing identity can become a fixed point that stymies the growth of the writer and contributes to imposter syndrome. For example, a student who reads her poetry at a local open mic thinks, "I've arrived. I'm a poet!" but then later, when she's sitting in her bedroom struggling to write a poem for English class, she may think, "Am I a poet?"

I invited students to draw a graphic that illustrated the spectrum of all the kinds of writers they could think of. Then they dropped a sticker down on where they thought their "writing brand" existed.

Students interpreted the assignment in different ways. Eliza drew "The Great Ferris Wheel of Writers," where writers occupied different bucket seats (Figure 4–2). She included "writers who write about their troubled past," "edgy poets," and "geeky fantasy writers." Where did Eliza find herself? On the "writers who don't write" bucket, which were "writers who think about what they could write instead of writing."

Regan drew a tree. At the root were "writers who write only to heal themselves" followed by "writers who write for the fun of it" followed by "writers

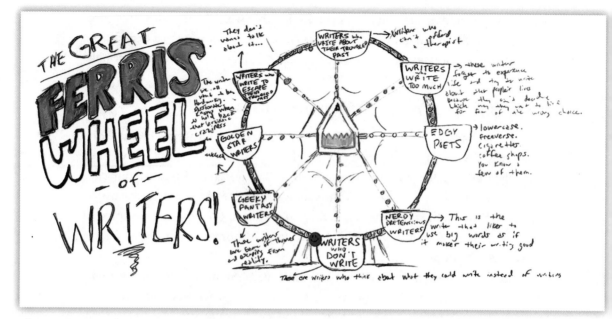

Figure 4–2 ~ *Eliza's Ferris Wheel of Writers*

who tell a story they know needs to be told" followed by the very tip-top of the tree where "writers who write just when people will see it" sat. She dropped her sticker between the first two rungs.

Kailie drew an actual line, even though she conceded that a writer's self-conception or public perception or literary merit was not linear (see Figure 4–3). The progression from left to right reads, "People who write words; People who write words often; People who write words often and are good at it; People who call themselves writers; Quite good writers; Amazing writers; People who make a career out of writing; Famous writers; Plath, Ginsberg and, like, Frost, I guess." This graphic brings up a lot of interesting questions: Does one grow as a writer when one moves from anonymity to fame? Can one make a career out of writing without being famous? Is fame the goal? Is name recognition the goal? Kailie dropped her My Little Pony sticker right between "People who call themselves writers" and "Quite good writers."

This activity brought out a rich discussion about defining yourself as a particular kind of writer versus possessing a writing identity as well as the nature of fame with regard to publishing. Instead of attaching writing identity to a

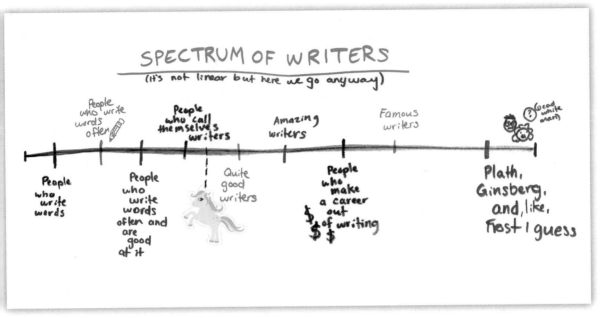

Figure 4–3 ~ *Kailie's Spectrum of Writers*

particular genre of writing, they decided, it was better to develop your writerly self-regard that transfers agency and autonomy no matter what form of writing you do, no matter who does or does not read it, and whether it is or is not published in the traditional sense.

Building Writerly Self-Regard

Writing from your own identity—your own place and history—and from your own experience on topics you are passionate about is the first step in developing writerly self-regard. To respect your own ideas and your own way of thinking is an essential part of building an identity as a writer. Observing and noticing your own life first and the lives of others around you is how you look at the world like a writer.

To help students begin to look at the world in this manner and develop an observational habit, I invite them to track their writing exigencies for one week.

In rhetorical discourse, *exigence* means "what is needed;" it's derived from the Latin word *exigentia*, meaning "urgency" (Bitzer 1968, 11). Sometimes we act on the world with our personal need for expression, like telling someone you love them. Sometimes the world acts on us, like when your science teacher assigns a yearlong research project. Both of these opportunities constitute an exigency to write, a rhetorical situation.

Essayist David Sedaris finds many of his essay topics in the small everyday stories he records in his diary. "I have a whole file on my computer about things I'd always wanted to write about. They're vignettes, little things that happened" (Strawser 2013, 43). Keeping a list of ideas, stories, characters, snippets of poetry, snippets of dialogue is a habit most writers maintain.

For this activity, students kept a running list of assigned writing and spontaneous writing for one school week, Monday through Friday. Assigned writing was any time someone asked them to write something: a teacher assigned a paper, a parent asked for their Christmas list, a club sponsor asked for their bio, or a college asked for an admission essay. Along with this list, they kept a list of writing opportunities and topics they spontaneously discovered, topics the universe mysteriously placed in front of them.

When we shared at the end of the week, we drew two columns on the board: assigned writing tasks and spontaneous writing opportunities. Under the assigned column, we found pretty typical offerings: Eliza's admission essay for the Common App, Alec's speech for another class, Nicholas' assignment to write an op-ed for his current events class, Sarah's argument about metal detectors in her Advanced Placement English class.

But the discovered or spontaneous writing list was longer and varied. Sarah's nephew asked her to read Crockett Johnson's *Harold and the Purple Crayon* to him; from this, she was inspired her to write an epic poem about a self-destructive man who had the power to draw the realities of his own life; for Katherine, it was the stories she heard when she accompanied her mother to Alcoholics Anonymous meetings. For Griffin, it was playing *Fate/Grand Order* and wanting to analyze its elements more in depth.

For Promise and Taylor, it was looking through pictures of their summer vacations that sparked an urgency to write. Taylor, who had traveled to France with our school's French Club, said she wanted to "write it for my future self, so I can look back and remember all of these great stories from that trip." Promise visited Africa, where her father was born. She said, "I want to write a chapbook that will relay my experiences, my newfound heritage, and the history of my new home."

In other words, exigencies happen. And writers who look at the world like writers are poised to catch, identify, and pin them to the wall. Selecting one's own topics and ideas for writing is perhaps the most critical part of developing writerly self-regard, allowing students to demonstrate agency and self-respect. Besides choosing their own topics and subjects to write about, there are a few other activities that help students build writerly self-regard: claiming their writing habits, rituals, writing space and time, skills, and mentors.

Claiming Your Habits

There is no end to conflicting advice out there for young writers. Although imitation and mentorship are a great way to learn how to write, students should figure out what works best for them as a writer. In *The Paris Review*, Toni Morrison says, "I tell my students one of the most important things they need to know is when they are their best creatively. They need to ask themselves, 'What does the ideal room look like? Is there music? Is there silence? Is there chaos outside or is there serenity outside? What do I need in order to release my imagination?'" (Gourevitch 2007, 358).

For every writing tip or technique you discover online, the next article will claim that technique doesn't work. For example, a lot of writers swear by outlining, but in his autobiography, *The Youngest Science,* science writer Lewis Thomas (1995) says it didn't work for him. "I changed the method to no method at all . . . and wrote without outline or planning in advance, as fast as I could. This worked better, or at least was more fun, and I was able to get started" (89).

Another piece of writing advice given to young writers is to write every day. Yet Toni Cade Bambara says as a young writer, her writing was sporadic and unscheduled. "I would simply commandeer time, space, paper, and pen, close the door, unplug the phone, get ugly with would-be intruders, and get to work for a few days" (Tate 1985, 215).

Writing is an idiosyncratic process. There are as many writing habits as there are writers. The trick is to help students figure out what works best for them instead of having all students process their work in the exact same way. I like to show students a variety of writing habits and rituals from professional writers, then ask them to jot down their own habits. Some students, of course, will have no writing habits, but having none is a habit itself.

When you sit down to write, how do you get started? Some writers outline their thoughts; some write without planning. Some draft in longhand but others compose digitally. What are some of the writing habits that help you in the writing process? Make a list of all the habits you've depended on in the past to help you write.

Stephen King famously writes two thousand words a day; James Joyce, ninety (Ang 2020). Reynolds Price had a daily quota of twenty-seven lines on a legal pad because twenty-seven lines added up to one typed page (Murray 1990, 60). Why do you think a daily word count is a writing habit of so many famous writers? Do you write daily? Do you have a daily word count? How would meeting a daily word count help or hinder you as a writer?

Claiming Your Rituals

Developing a writing ritual can also develop writerly self-regard. Some rituals are as simple as creating an environment to write, then selecting a dedicated time and honoring the time and space with the practice of writing. Similar to creating a habit, a ritual can trigger the writing state of mind. If students write mostly at home, they can practice rituals, such as listening to music, locking their little brother out of their bedroom, or just getting out a special pencil and notebook.

Just like writing habits, no one ritual works for every writer. Although many writers listen to music while they write, it didn't work for E. B. White, who said in *The Paris Review*, "I never listen to music when I'm working. I haven't that kind of attentiveness, and I wouldn't like it at all" (Gourevitch 2009a, 137). In his *Paris Review* interview, Haruki Murakami said, "When I'm in writing mode for a novel, I get up at four a.m. and work for five to six hours. In the afternoon, I run for ten kilometers or swim for fifteen hundred meters (or do both), then I read a bit and listen to some music. I go to bed at nine p.m." (Gourevitch 2009b, 350).

Four teachers in the Louisiana Writing Project investigated rituals as effective classroom practice (O'Shaughnessy et al. 2002) and found that time limits on writing tasks and the repetition of a writing practice during the same time and same place every day made writing a normal, nonthreatening activity for students. Do you have any writing rituals in your classroom that your students participate in? What are some writing rituals you would like to introduce as part of your classroom practice? If you allow students to have sustained writing time as part of your daily class time, spend some time discussing three or four classroom rituals that signal to students that writing is about to commence.

Classroom Writing Rituals

- Listen to music: Music helps some writers relax into the mind space necessary to create. Create a playlist of writing songs on Spotify and queue it up as a signal to the brain it's time to write. Make sure to use ear pods to not disturb the other writers in the room.

- Read a poem: Creativity begets creativity. Before I write fiction or poetry, I often read for ten or fifteen minutes to get my head in a literary headspace. Keep a folder of poems, short stories, or essays on your Google Drive that will inspire you to write.

- Get comfortable: If the classroom offers both traditional and nontraditional seating, allow students to select their physical space for writing. This small gesture goes a long way toward building their writing autonomy.

- Turn off phones: Although a phone can be a great aid when researching or jotting down those exigencies of the moment, when it comes time to write for a sustained time, a digital device can be more of a distraction than a service.

- Select the right instruments: Choose a dedicated journal or notebook or folder in Google Drive to keep writing in. Some writers prefer Moleskine notebooks for gathering story ideas and their laptop for drafting. I have a number of journals that all serve different purposes: a dream journal, a running journal, a writing journal, and a journal where I track books I've read. When it's time to draft a piece of writing, I almost always write a first draft on a legal pad, then transcribe it to a Google Doc later.

- Set minigoals: Some students need to set minigoals for themselves as part of their writing ritual. Setting small work goals and meeting them will help students build writerly self-regard. Keeping a promise to yourself around a positive habit is essential to maintaining the habit and forming self-respect. I encourage students to ask themselves: *What two things do I need to work on today? What is one obtainable writing goal I can finish in the next thirty minutes of writing time?*

- Set a time limit: During NaNoWriMo (National Novel Writing Month), my students liked to do writing sprints—five-, ten-, fifteen-minute blocks of time—to write as much as they could as quickly as they could. Although these short bursts of writing might not make it to the final draft, they often allow writers to break through the resistance of perfectionism to some literary gold.

Claiming Your Space and Time

Screenwriter Leslie Dixon (*Mrs. Doubtfire, The Thomas Crown Affair*) writes in a screened in back porch and Amy Holden Jones (*Mystic Pizza, Maid to Order*) writes in a zero-gravity chair, looking out a window directly down a canyon toward the ocean (Iglesias 2001, 85). Edith Wharton, I learned during a tour of her home, The Mount, wrote in bed all morning, dropping longhand written pages of her novels on the floor for her maid to pick up. Dalton Trumbo (Trex 2009) wrote in a bath tub, Geraldine Brooks (2001) on "a tankard-scoured tavern table that once saw service in an 18th-century inn," and Maya Angelou checked into a hotel room and instructed the staff to remove all decorations and paintings off the wall so she could settle in and write (Charney 2017b).

Although some writers claim to be able to write anywhere, most writers have a special time and place they've dedicated to the act of writing. In the summertime, I write on my back porch; in the winter, I use a spare bedroom that serves as my office. There's something declarative and peaceful about cleaning a space and selecting a block of time to write that helps the writer get into that headspace.

Some writers write late at night, some in the early dawn. Some snatch a few minutes when they can. Writer Craig Morgan Teicher (2017) says, "I often write on my phone, and if I can get a couple of lines out during a smoke break at work—I work a nine-to-five, running the web operations of a magazine—then I'm good. Out of hundreds of fifteen-minute practice sessions over several years, a book is born" (39).

One of the best gifts we can offer students is to give protected, sustained writing time in class, then help them become aware of how they spend it. It's like cringing when your child blows his allowance on Five Nights at Freddy's plushies, knowing he will want a few dollars later when the ice-cream truck comes around. Blowing it is how kids figure out how to manage it. Giving students time to write and allowing them to squander it and figure out their own habits of writing is an invaluable gift of self-awareness.

When working on a writing project, my students sometimes have a full week or two of class periods (five to ten ninety-minute blocks) to work on their projects. To aid their time awareness, I ask students to fill out a Daily Work Log for one week that allows them to track how they spend their writing time.

I encourage them to write down everything they do even if it is "off task." Figures 4–4 and 4–5 are two examples from my class:

Activity	Start Time	End Time	Notes
Start the Day Off Write	10:03	10:21	I chose the fiction one.
Cried	10:21	10:45	Don't ask pls
Made a tik tok	10:45	11:01	Here's the TikTok URL in case you want to watch it.
Talked to K---	11:01	11:13	
Answered emails	11:13	11:28	

Figure 4–4 ~
Student A's Daily Work Log

Figure 4–5 ~
Student B's Daily Work Log

Activity	Start Time	End Time	Notes
Start the Day Off Write	10:03	10:20	I wrote about a girl named Cate.
Scripting on Heart Stopper	10:10	10:35	Wrote a scene with Avery and the officer
Asked R—to give me feedback on the intro	10:35	10:50	
Writing	10:53	11:16	
Went to the bathroom	11:16	11:20	

Once we finished this weeklong tracking activity, students analyzed how they spent their writing time and reflected on where the time went. Student A noticed that on days she was ensnared in social drama, she had a hard time concentrating on her writing. Student B observed when she had an ongoing project she was excited about, it was easier to get into the writing immediately. Both students agreed that having a dedicated writing time was helpful in developing a writing practice, but tracking the productivity inside that time was critical to understanding how they worked as writers.

Where do you like to write? Outside in a park, on the Starbucks patio, on the benches outside the public library? Or do you like to write inside—in your bedroom? At the dining room table? Do you find that where you write influences what or how you write? Why or why not?

4-3

Do you write on the weekends or in the summer? When is the best time for you to write? Late at night, after school, early in the morning? Do you find that when you write influences what or how you write? Why or why not?

4-4

Claiming Your Skills

One of the biggest builders of writerly self-regard is helping students develop basic writing skill. I once worked with a brilliant educator who taught math in rural eastern Kentucky. He could break down the most convoluted math principle in the simplest terms to the least interested students. One day I shared how I struggled with math in high school and how it impacted my confidence and interest.

"How do you teach kids to have confidence in a subject they don't care about?" I asked. His answer was simple: teach them basic number sense and build their confidence through skill acquisition. "We have it backward in education," he said. "We think we should build students' self-esteem first, then they'll be able to learn our content, but the exact opposite is true. Once they truly understand the content, they have self-esteem. Once a student has number sense, he can learn logic and abstract concepts, and that's power."

The same is true of writing. Helping students develop basic writing skills, including their faculties with language, grammar, and usage, builds a solid foundation for writerly self-regard. I use the handout in Figure 4–6 at the beginning of each writing project to help students set goals in relation to their writing skills.

4-5

Writers continually develop skills throughout their writing life. What is one writing skill you feel very confident of? What is one writing skill you could teach to another student? Where did you learn this skill? How does this skill help you as a writer?

4-6

Think back over the last two or three years of your life as a student writer. What is one writing skill you wish you could improve on? How could you learn this skill? From your teacher, a mentor text, a peer, a YouTube video, or a writing center? How would learning this skill benefit you as a writer?

Figure 4–6 ~ *Student Self-Skill Assessment*

Name:_____

Describe the writing project you would like to do for this unit. Please include the form you want to write in (speech, blog, memoir, essay, short story, poem, etc.) and a short summary of your idea.

Circle all the skills you currently have that will help you with this project:

Brainstorming   Journaling   Freewriting   Mapping   Drafting   Listing   Clustering
Narrowing Your Topic   Picturing Your Audience   Researching   Outlining   Plotting
Storyboarding   Organizing   Interviewing   Taking Notes   Finding Sources
Evaluating Sources   Paraphrasing   Fact Checking   Documenting Sources
Writing Effective Sentences   Writing Effective Paragraphs   Choosing Effective Words
Reading Out Loud   Revising   Editing   Inquiring   Getting Feedback
Proofreading for Spelling and Grammar

Circle all the skills you would like to develop during this project.

Brainstorming   Journaling   Freewriting   Mapping   Drafting   Listing   Clustering
Narrowing Your Topic   Picturing Your Audience   Researching   Outlining   Plotting
Storyboarding   Organizing   Interviewing   Taking Notes   Finding Sources
Evaluating Sources   Paraphrasing   Fact Checking   Documenting Sources
Writing Effective Sentences   Writing Effective Paragraphs   Choosing Effective Words
Reading Out Loud   Revising   Editing   Inquiring   Getting Feedback
Proofreading for Spelling and Grammar

Describe your writing project.

Claiming Your Mentors

Literacy researcher Alfred Tatum (2009) defines "textual lineage" as "a text that becomes a part of the student long after he reads it and leads him to think and act differently" (18). Reading regularly and widely serves to bolster writerly self-regard by exposing students to different styles and forms that serve as mentors and become part of that student's identity and lineage. Reading helps writers internalize language and grammar as well as showing them writerly risk-taking. When we read Eula Biss' (2007) essay "The Pain Scale," in which she arranges her essay along the zero to ten scale used by doctors to ascertain the pain patients are experiencing, Marley said, "Can we do that? I didn't know you could write an essay that way."

Reading also helps students see themselves in the wider world of letters. Even though she grew up in Jamaica, "a country full of black people," Nicole Dennis-Benn (2018) had never read a book written by a black writer, much less a black woman writer. "All the books we read were by white British authors. I never saw the details of my own life worth writing about; I never thought anyone would care" (106). One day when she was fifteen, she found a copy of Toni Morrison's (2004) *Beloved* discarded on a table in her school's library, and it changed her life. Reading a book written by or about a person who looks like you can have a huge impact on your ability to regard your own experiences as valid material for writing.

But reading is only one source of writing mentorship. Listening is another area where writers can learn to hear language they want to emulate on the page. Annie Prolux (1999) says, "I listen attentively in bars and cafes, while standing in line at the checkout counter, noting particular pronunciations and the rhythms of regional speech, vivid turns of speech and the duller talk of everyday life." And Wendell Berry says, "A major part of my schooling as a writer came from the conversation of 'uneducated' farmers" (House 2020).

When Gayl Jones was a young writer in Lexington, Kentucky, she told her junior-year English teacher, "I want to write like Henry James." But she also spent weekends on her grandmother's small farm in Fayette County, where she listened to the stories of her family. "The best of my writing comes from having *heard* rather than having read," Jones said. "In the beginning, *all* of the richness came from people rather than books" (Baker 2020).

Teachers are another category of mentors. Looking back over my life, in addition to Mrs. Toadvine and Ms. Umfress, I was fortunate to learn from at least a dozen teachers who helped me become a better writer and thinker. I have also learned from my peers, from my writing group, and from craft books. Students may cite teachers from their past who helped them become writers, but they also may cite friends, family, YouTube videos, peer tutors at the Writing Center or anyone who has advised and supported their writing.

> Think back over your reading life. Are there books that have formed your identity, books that are part of your "textual lineage"? In *The African-American Guide to Writing and Publishing Nonfiction*, Jewell Parker Rhodes writes a whole chapter on the importance of literary ancestors, the writers who are like your literary grandmothers and grandfathers. Who are your literary ancestors? What writers have you learned from and enjoyed? Why do you claim them as an ancestor?

4-7

> Think back over your writing life. What teachers come to mind as mentors of your writing skill? Can you think of a particular lesson that a teacher taught that improved your writing? What other mentors have you had as a writer? Have you mentored someone in writing yourself?

4-8

> David Sedaris said he found his voice by imitating other people, trying on the voices of Joan Didion and Raymond Carver, for example. "It's all part of discovering what you sound like. I think we all do that—we take a little bit of this, and a little bit of that, and we just kind of put it in a big kettle, and we find ourselves" (Strawser 2013, 46). What mentors have you found through reading? Are there writers you have imitated in style or voice? What mentor texts do you find yourself returning to over and over? Why?

4-9

Declaring Yourself as a Writer

During the summer of 2003, I participated in the South Louisiana Writing Project's New Orleans Writing Walkabout led by Southeastern Louisiana University writing professor Richard Louth. It was a fantastic (and hellishly hot) day of writing and walking and eating and drinking. Early in the morning, about twenty-five writers met in the lobby of Le Richelieu Hotel on Chartres Street and broke up into small groups. Before we launched out into our day, Louth told us a story about a group of Mississippi writers on a walkabout who attempted to gain access to a college football stadium that was under construction. "No, I don't have the authority to let you in," the foreman said. But then they said, "We're writers!" And he said, "Well then, come on in. There's an open gate around the corner" (Louth 2002).

This story bears witness to the power of declaration. Before our New Orleans trek, Louth asked each of us to turn to someone and introduce ourselves this way: "Hi, my name is Liz and I'm a writer." We felt a bit goofy and summer-campy, but the statement did create a tingly affirmation about our ambitions. Louth (2002) says that declaring yourself a writer opens all kinds of doors because "writers who believe in themselves tap into an unimaginable power; people sense this, and treat them with the kind of reverence often given to priests."

I've included this introductory ritual in all the writing walkabouts I've hosted, and students laugh and exaggerate the practice, but it's amazing how merely declaring themselves as writers goes a long way to establishing the fact. One caveat: declaring yourself a writer only holds power if you already conceive of yourself as such, but a statement like "I'm a writer" may make some students who have no writerly self-regard feel worse. They may feel like they are lying to and about themselves (Wood, Perunovic, and Lee 2009).

Kentucky teacher Lisa Wheeler uses writing walkabouts for a cross-discipline writing activity that teaches economics and local history with her middle school students in Paintsville, a small town of four thousand. "It's amazing what happens when my students walk around town. They will see people they know, who ask, 'What are you doing?' and the students respond, 'We're writers!' Everyone is happy with that answer" (2004).

Declaring yourself a writer can be shored up by developing a writing practice. This practice can be as simple as jotting down a few sentences about your day in a notebook. Three years ago, a friend got me a ten-year journal, and it only has five lines in it for each day of the year for a decade. I like how the constraint of just five lines makes my entries concise and necessary. Wringing only the essential parts from my day and then recording them in the journal increases my observational skills and my ability to summarize and to write concisely.

Figure 4–7 ~ *Three Sentences × Thirty Days*

Objectives: Build writing fluency, generate writing ideas, practice looking at your life like a writer, practice summarizing, practice detail selection.

Instructions: Every day for thirty days, write two sentences to record one experience. Choose either a significant experience, like the arrival of a baby brother, or something insignificant, like watching some ducks swim in a pond. Allow the constraint of writing only two sentences to bring clarity and brevity to your observation.

Day 1	Day 15
Day 2	Day 16
Day 3	Day 17
Day 4	Day 18
Day 5	Day 19
Day 6	Day 20
Day 7	Day 21
Day 8	Day 22
Day 9	Day 23
Day 10	Day 24
Day 11	Day 25
Day 12	Day 26
Day 13	Day 27
Day 14	Day 28
	Day 29
	Day 30

Look back over your thirty days of three-sentence observations. What patterns emerge? What writing topics leap out at you? What experiences deserve exploring more in depth? Which of these experiences would you like to write about? Why?

PART
THREE

Developing Writing Courage

Fear of
the Blank Page

ow that we've examined our writing history, unpacked some attitudes about writing, and created an awareness of our writing preferences and processes, it's time to investigate the social and emotional barriers that shut down the writing process before it gets started. Normalizing these fears as part of everyone's writing process helps students see their own anxiety, not as something that means they're ill equipped to write, but as evidence that they *are* writers.

Students who don't write aren't beset by fears of writing. Students bravely trying to match an experience with language will face the discomfort that creation brings. As Brown (2012) writes in *Daring Greatly*, "When we make the choice to dare greatly, we sign up to get our asses kicked. We can choose courage or we can choose comfort, but we can't have both. Not at the same time" (56). Getting your ass kicked by a piece of writing is part of the process.

Last month, the editor of a magazine I freelance for called to see if I'd be interested in writing an article about coffee shops in small towns. I agreed. We discussed angles the story might take. I started thinking about the article, imagining an opening sentence, a cool closing sequence, a couple of frames that might work for organization. I was brimming with ideas. Later that day, I made a cup of tea and went up to my office, ready to type up a draft of the article. I sat down to deliver the goods.

A blank Word document. Deep breath. Hands on keys. What was that opening sentence I wanted to use?

Hmm . . . should I buy another pair of black boots this winter since my favorite ones are getting dumpy in the heels? Should I start running in the morning instead of waiting until after school? Earlier at Tardy Table, Mrs. McClanahan laughed at something I said; had she been laughing *with* me or *at* me? Also where is my pound cake recipe?

I wrestled my attention back to the page. There it was, waiting for me as immaculate and as expansive as it was ten minutes ago.

Wow, I thought. That document was really blank.

"Coffee Shop Article." I typed. Click. File. Click. Save.

Hours earlier I had written the article in my head, yet now I couldn't think of a single word. What do I have to say about coffee shops in a small town? Nothing. Well, I once worked at a coffee shop in a small town. I typed, "I once worked at a coffee shop in a small town." Ridiculous. The beginning of a Hallmark Christmas special. I deleted the sentence.

Let's see what's out there about small towns and coffee shops. National Geographic had "These Unexpected Cities Have the Best Coffee in the US." I flipped through their slideshow until I got to Greenville, South Carolina's Spill the Beans. Adorable, I thought. I clicked on the hyperlink, which took me to their website. There's an embedded map. I clicked on the directions and entered our home address. Five hours to Greenville. What a cute downtown. Oh, there's a B&B called the Swamp Rabbit Inn. Very funky. Click. Click. Click.

You know how this ends. I closed the computer. My blank page would be waiting there for the next round of dancing tomorrow.

"Did you get started on your piece?" my husband said when I came back downstairs.

"Sort of," I said. "You wanna watch *Jeopardy!*?"

What Is It?

Writing anything—a short wedding toast for your cousin, an email to your boss, an essay for a graduate class—invites existential fear. Some writers have likened it to standing on an empty stage, alone, with nothing to say, while facing an audience. Or a firing squad.

When the page is blank, anything and everything is possible. Marring the pristine page feels like a desecration, a walk through new fallen snow. Do we dare disturb the universe with our imperfect scratches at meaning? If writing is an exercise of vision and choice, then making the wrong choice spoils the vision. We intellectually know a first draft can be revised, but that doesn't stop our heart from lying to us about the stakes of wrong turns.

All writers have felt this distress. In an interview from *The Paris Review*, Joan Didion says, "Writing fiction is, for me, a fraught business, an occasion of daily dread for at least the first half of the novel, and sometimes all the way through" (Gourevitch 2006, 475). When student writers experience blank page anxiety, they may think they're alone in this dread, that no one else in the history of writing was so much of a loser as to not be able to write a single word. They often compound the anxiety by beating themselves up, engaging in a self-defeating inner monologue that deadlocks them further. And they fail to do the one thing that could decrease the anxiety: writing. And many develop the evil triad of writing sabotage: writer's block, procrastination, and perfectionism.

In my senior writing class, which operates as a writing community with several protected days of uninterrupted studio time to create and write, I noticed three distinct patterns of behavior during our writing days. The students all tumbled in as the tardy bell rang at 10:02 a.m. A few of them immediately grabbed their Chromebooks, pulled out their daily work logs, and started to write. No preamble. No fuss. Just sat down and got after it.

Another larger subset needed time to ease into the class. They found their seats, then wandered around bothering other like-minded individuals or fixed themselves a cup of coffee or spent some time selecting the right playlist. That ritual lasted until around 10:15 a.m. Once started, they were as industrious as the first group.

But the last group truly struggled. Even with cues like the tardy bell, the other students' typing, the silence in the room, they still needed external nudges. I passed by their desks at 10:20, then again at 10:30, maybe again at 10:45.

"Hey, what's on the agenda today?" I might start out. They would pull out their daily work log, and sometimes get to work. Or not. Nothing seemed to produce the inspiration or the conditions in which they could write. Sometimes they asked me to step out into the hall; sometimes they cried.

"I'm just not a good writer."

"Who said that?" I looked around, pretending to be offended.

"Nobody." They wiped their eyes. I tried to draw them out. Then we talked about the lies we tell ourselves. Namely that good writers come in and sit down and get after it because they know what they want to say and how they want to say it.

That is a lie, I reminded them.

But those first few kids *looked* like they knew what they were doing, they *looked* like they knew what they wanted to say and how to say it. To my students who could not settle in, it seemed like those other kids had something they didn't: writing talent.

Nothing could be farther from the truth. The students who couldn't find their groove were just as voracious readers, writers, and thinkers as those stop-drop-and-write writers. What they didn't have, however, was a way to manage their anxiety in order to practice their writing. They needed a strategy to withstand the initial agony of not having the right words.

The first set of students had figured out that writing was a time hustle: to start early enough to plan and write or write the crappy draft quickly to craft later. For a host of reasons, both personal and institutional, many students never get to that point where they can "craft" an essay. And it's in revision where the real gains in writing proficiency occur.

We often write in reaction to the circumstances of not knowing what to say and how to say it, coupled with the time crunch that procrastination has jammed us into. Instead of writing according to a proactive plan—a plan that takes into account research, drafting, *and* the inner resistance to get started—we often wait until the last minute, then panic write just to get it done. We may be dissatisfied with the results, but so happy the discomfort has been alleviated.

For neurodivergent students, the path may not be as simple or direct. Telling these students to "try harder" or "stop wasting time" adds to their shame as being seen as irresponsible and adds frustration to the anxiety they already feel. These students may need additional support, such as using physical counters to track time, writing down a specific schedule of smaller tasks, built-in planning or doodling time. They may need to double the time to complete a task.

Some students had figured out if they sketched out a wonky outline or wrote a hot mess first draft quickly, they could bank the time needed to read it over and over again plus write it over and over again until it semimatched what they semiwanted it to say. Or ditch it completely and start all over. And *that*—fortifying themselves in the face of inadequacy and buying themselves time to revise and create—seemed to be their talent.

> Most writers feel anxiety or fear when they start to write. What does it feel like when you have blank page in front of you? Do you feel excitement or dread? Or a mix of both? What tricks have you used to get started on a writing assignment?

5-1

> Do you avoid writing tasks or do you jump right in and get started? If you avoid writing, how does the avoidance serve your writing goals? If you jump right in, how does this strategy serve your writing goals?

5-2

> In Elizabeth Gilbert's (2015) *Big Magic*, she says fear and creativity are conjoined twins sharing the same womb, the same birthday, and a few vital organs. If you kill the fear, she contends, you also kill the creativity. "So I don't try to kill off my fear. I don't go to war against it. Instead, I make all that space for it. It seems to me that the less I fight my fear, the less it fights back. If I can relax, fear relaxes too" (25). Do you make space for your fear of the blank page? What techniques have you found for relaxing with fear instead of fighting against it? How could you model this technique for your students?

5-1

How Does It Feel?

Whether you're a student with an assigned topic or a *New York Times* journalist with a deadline, a couple of feelings present themselves at the point of composition. One is the fear of failure: *I won't be able to do this* or *I won't be able to do this well.* Two is the dread of the work itself: *This is going to take forever, and I dread it like a root canal.*

One difference between the student writer and the *Times* reporter is the length of time between feeling the fear and starting to write. With the *Times* reporter, only a few minutes may elapse. The deadline is in their face, and they must respond. They respond by sitting down and writing.

Students may feel the fear and look at their syllabus. The due date is two weeks away. They have other classes, a job, extracurriculars, a family, and a social life. They can afford to put it off a few more days. And a few days more.

And a few days more. Until they can't. There's a tipping point, of course, when the fear of not meeting a deadline overwhelms the fear of starting. At that point, a writer feels the aforementioned fears coupled now with panic.

And your body prepares you for the threat it now perceives as a life-threatening emergency. Your mental acuity sharpens, your blood sugar goes up, your heart pumps blood into your muscles readying them for action. You may begin to breath faster, you zero in on the blank page, your mouth goes dry, and your stomach churns as you break into a sweat. You hunch over the laptop like a warrior gearing up for battle. Swift intake of breath. Charge!

A little brain science here: primitive humans evolved to react to a beastie jumping from the tall grasses. Even though a five-page term paper is no saber-toothed tiger, we respond as if it were. We imagine these intellectual problems to be vital problems of life or death. The prefrontal cortex, which helps students plan, concentrate, and retrieve memories, is then hijacked by the older regions of the brain, such as the amygdala, which has evolved to protect us.

Making up a third of the human cortex, the prefrontal cortex, which also keeps a lid on our emotions and impulses, doesn't even reach full maturity until students are in college (Arsten, Mazure, and Sinha 2021) and it's vulnerable even to regular daily stressors, like missing the bus or forgetting a lunch box. Staying on task, storing memory, and thinking abstractly are needed when a student begins a writing task, but if the task is perceived as a threat, the prefrontal cortex is shut down, the amygdala and our limbic system are alerted, and the body is flooded with stress hormones. This is a simplified rendering of the very complex neurochemical and physical response to stress, but research demonstrates that the very thing we use to write, namely our prefrontal cortex, will "stop firing after being exposed to a flood of stress hormones" (Arsten, Mazure, and Sinha 2021, 17). Factor in the chronic stress that students with adverse childhood experiences struggle with, and it's not hard to understand why starting a writing task presents a nearly insurmountable obstacle.

Psychologists break down anxiety into three interrelated processes: physiological, cognitive, and behavioral (Siegel 2010, 108–9). When a student has a writing assignment, he might feel cognitive anxiety (*I'm stupid. I can't write. People will make fun of me.*) coupled with physiological anxiety (racing heart, sweaty palms), which results in an avoidant behavior (*I'm going to watch TikTok for three hours*). Someone who experiences cognitive and physiological anxiety seeks relief by putting distance between themselves and the source of their anxiety. This delay may be short-lived, but we repeat it over and over because it makes the anxiety, even for a little while, go away.

As a writing teacher for three decades, I can report that many of my students have convinced themselves they write better under this pressure. They may even unconsciously procrastinate to produce the body's fight-or-flight response to battle the imaginary threat of a writing assignment. Some feel like they can't write unless they get that bump. Some carry this dysfunctional bond with them from middle school to high school to graduate school and beyond.

> Do you ever feel as though when you sit down to write you'll have nothing to say? That your mind will go blank? Have you ever had this feeling? What did it feel like? Why does starting a writing assignment create anxiety in writers?

5-3

> In *Draft No. 4*, a collection of eight essays on the writing process, John McPhee (2017) says even after he became a *New Yorker* staff writer, he had misgivings about his abilities. "You would think that by then I would have developed some confidence in writing a new story, but I hadn't, and never would. To lack confidence at the outset seems rational to me. It doesn't matter that something you've done before worked out well. Your last piece is never going to write your next one for you" (19). How does a lack of confidence in your own writing seem like a reasonable response to a writing task? Do you agree or disagree that "it doesn't matter that something you've done before worked out well"?

5-2

How Does It Manifest in Writers?

Even though the telling of our stories and declaring of our truths is one of the most fulfilling human experiences we can engage in, the neurological elements that must be in harmony to make it happen exhaust me from the outset. It's a task many writers have responded to with predictable maladies. I have experienced these myself and witnessed them in my writing colleagues and my students. The three most common stress responses to starting a writing project are writer's block, procrastination, and perfectionism.

Writer's Block

The essential act of writing—creating something from nothing—is a Herculean mental feat necessitating hundreds of emotional and physical acts. In some writers, the crushing weight of creation staunches even the tiniest trickle of thought. They feel physically and intellectually gridlocked. In *The Midnight Disease*, Alice W. Flaherty points out that writers who are blocked have two common characteristics: "they do not write despite being intellectually capable of doing so, and they suffer because they are not writing" (80). For some writers, the suffering may be the point; for others, writer's block is just a lack of creative will. As James Boswell and Samuel Johnson cavorted around Scotland on tour, Boswell marveled that Johnson seemed to be able to write in any circumstance: "I wondered to see him write so much so easily. He verified his own doctrine that 'a man may always write when he will set himself doggedly to it'" (157).

We didn't even have a name for it until 1947, when psychiatrist Edmund Bergler named it "writer's block." For a fascinating deep dive into the machinations of creative blocks, I recommend Zachary Leader's *Writer's Block* as he tracks the infamous blockages of Samuel Coleridge, William Wordsworth, and Mark Twain while also examining how writer's block may, in fact, be internalized as "institutionalized prohibitions . . . of class, sex, and race" (232).

For some writers, a blockage at the beginning of a project may be part of their process, a familiar creative mile marker ending with breakthroughs and revelations. For others, like Johnson, blocks aren't creative barriers, but evidence of lack of skill or vision or confidence. When poet Danez Smith finds the words not flowing, he asks himself a series of questions: "Why am I stuck? Is it the piece? Am I feeling balanced enough in other areas in my life . . . ? Am I hungry? Am I tired? Are the idea and the genre of what I'm working on agreeing with each other? Am I experiencing a roadblock or a directive to try something else?" (Temple 2017).

The notion of a creative who is "blocked" has existed for as long as writers, artists, and musicians have been trying to express themselves. And whether you believe writer's block is a real malady or not, you may have experienced trouble getting the ideas in your head out on the page.

Have you experienced writer's block before? What did it feel like? What was the occasion of the block, and how did you resolve it? If you haven't experienced it, what do you do to get started writing? How would you help someone who is experiencing writer's block?

5-4

Contemporary novelist Jodi Picoult dismisses the idea of writer's block. "Think about it—when you were blocked in college and had to write a paper, didn't it always manage to fix itself the night before the paper was due? Writer's block is having too much time on your hands. If you have a limited amount of time to write, you just sit down and do it" (Charney 2017a). Do you agree or disagree that writer's block is just a matter of having too much time on your hands? What personal experience with writer's block informed your answer?

5-3

Psychology Today poses five reasons why a writer might experience writer's block: "You've lost your way; your passion has waned; your expectations are too high; you're burned out; you're too distracted" (Reynolds 2015). I've experienced all of these, sometimes at the same time. Has any one of these blocked you before? Which one? How did you get beyond it? What strategies did you learn to model for students?

5-4

Procrastination

You might say writer's block is just procrastination that's taken up residence and unpacked its bags. When you're dodging a writing task, everything becomes an emergency that needs to be taken care of. For teachers, it might be grading, planning, documenting, which is never caught up. For students, it might be other homework, practicing a sport, or even, yes, chores. For me, I often feel compelled into a flurry of cleaning. Anything to put off the task of writing.

The literary world is rife with writers who delivered genius first novels, then struggled for decades to produce a second work; the academic world too is stuffed with scholars who put off the writing of their dissertation for months and years. Procrastination among entrepreneurs, inventors, and artists has birthed a whole subculture of accountability coaches and support groups to help creatives battle their inner demons of delay.

Not everyone thinks procrastination is a bad thing. University of San Diego professor Frank Partnoy (2012) maintains in *Wait: The Art and Science of Delay* that waiting until the last minute to do something is smart. Learning to delay the decision-making process conserves energy, and we often make better decisions if we delay them until the last possible minute. Strategic delay gives you time to assimilate new knowledge or to develop an idea before launching into the writing.

Even though my students groan and blame themselves—*Ugh, I'm so lazy*—procrastination as protracted laziness is a myth. I've met dozens of brilliant, committed, studious students who were ambitious and productive: they all procrastinated. I, too, as an adult with total awareness of the stakes of putting off a task continue to do so, even as I have become less and less dependent on this coping mechanism as I have learned more about why I do it and the role procrastination plays in my writing process.

Some students procrastinate by actively avoiding the work and distracting themselves with something pleasurable, and some procrastinate unconsciously by doing things that look like work. The difference between motion and action—the writer may look like she's swimming (action), but she's really just treading water (motion) and not going anywhere.

My student Alec clearly understood that procrastination and its attendant indifference helped him avoid the fear of failure. He writes: "I suppose I use procrastination in my writing in a negative way, if I write things I don't really put much effort into, this way, when people criticize my piece, it really doesn't matter. I don't like it either. This isn't something I purposefully do, but it is usually a by-product of procrastination."

In *Embarrassment*, Tom Newkirk (2017) calls this the "posture of indifference" (61), which can be a necessary attitude to assume when one has procrastinated out of fear and then received poor scores on the performance. Psychologists call this "self-handicapping," sabotaging your performance on a task to give yourself an excuse. As a teacher, I noticed students who are gifted often self-sabotage in the very area they've been identified as gifted.

When a student doesn't try and still performs well, she might assume the outcome is based on luck, or exceptionalism, or perhaps her uncanny ability to game the system. This response will lessen her growth as a writer as well. She may interpret success at writing as just a fluke or something that is destined for some and not for others, instead of a skill that can be learned, practiced, and achieved.

> Do you procrastinate writing assignments? If you do, are you more of an active procrastinator, doing something else like researching, or are you more of a passive procrastinator, avoiding the task of writing altogether? How does procrastination benefit or harm you? If you don't procrastinate, what are some of the strategies you use to get started with a writing task?

5-5

> In writer and blogger Tim Urban's (2016) TED talk "Inside the Mind of a Master Procrastinator," Urban introduces us to the three voices in every procrastinator's mind: The Rational Decision Maker, The Instant Gratification Monkey, and The Panic Monster. Using his own story of putting off his ninety-page senior thesis until three days before it was due, Urban explains how the mind of the procrastinator works. Watch this fifteen-minute talk at https://www.ted.com/talks/tim_urban_inside_the_mind_of_a_master_procrastinator. Do you identify with Urban's story? What are your big takeaways from this TED talk?

5-6

> Students need large blocks of dedicated class time to develop a writing idea, narrow their topic, outline or draft, and get feedback and revise. But that time can be unproductive if students are actively or passively procrastinating. Do you talk about ways to battle procrastination and self-sabotage? How do you balance the need for valuable unstructured writing time with its potential to trigger procrastination in some students?

5-5

Perfectionism

Brown (2012) writes "perfectionism is not the path that leads us to our gifts and to our sense of purpose; it's a hazardous detour" (128). Most students know perfectionism is a dead-end detour promising to lead somewhere, yet they don't know how to stop taking that same street over and over.

Many parents of gifted kids like to tell me their children are perfectionists, and they beam as if that equates with achievement. But perfectionists aren't necessarily striving for a goal; they may be protecting their self-worth by avoiding anything risky. The perfectionists in the room often defer to subjects that are easy or that they've written about before so they can "perfectly" write about the subject. Some of my most difficult writing conferences are when I have invited students to create something of personal value, but they just want to figure out "what you're looking for," so they can dominate or crush the task at hand. To write a successful draft of anything, one must first be willing to fail at the first couple (or thirty-seven) drafts to make it work. Without risking failure, students often choose safe subjects or limited tasks or rewrite the same essay over and over.

Perfectionism often seeks distraction to numb itself from the pain of trying something new. Social media exploits that moment when you can't figure out what you want to say and the blank page mocks you. When you're staring at the wall with your brain whirling—*How do I say this? What am I doing?*—the social media dopamine fix is so seductive. But the Twitter check never helps. It merely distracts, then anesthetizes, and ultimately heightens the anxiety.

Another way in which perfectionism shuts down writers is the desire for perfect circumstances in which to write. Everything must be perfect if the writing is to be perfect, we tell ourselves. I struggle with this. I feel dependent on the just-right pen, the right notebook, the right tea at the right temperature, and two days of nothing scheduled stretched out in front of me. Even the arriving mail can break this idyllic spell of writing I'm conjuring.

5-7 Essayist Rebecca Solnit writes, "So many of us believe in perfection, which ruins everything else, because the perfect is not only the enemy of the good; it's also the enemy of the realistic, the possible, and the fun" (Gilbert 2015, 166). Do you agree or disagree with this statement? Do you or someone you know suffer from perfectionism? Has it ruined the real, the possible, and the fun you might have had with writing? Why or why not?

5-8 Student writer Maggie writes about her expectations at the beginning of a writing project: "The hardest part of writing is being okay with what I've written. Right now, my vision is so clear but I'm already worried that what comes out on the page isn't going to be what I am picturing right now and it never is and I know it never will be. So I have to continue to struggle with myself and convince myself that what I've written is enough and good in itself." Have you ever felt the way Maggie feels? How do you keep going even when what you see on the page isn't what you wanted to see? How do you convince yourself that what you are writing is good enough?

When you share your writing with students, do you feel pressure for it to be perfect? In what way would showing your students imperfect drafts of your own writing lift the burden of their own struggles with perfectionism? In what way might sharing be a risk for you?

5–6

Brown (2012) writes, "Perfectionism is self-destructive simply because perfection doesn't exist. It's an unattainable goal" (33). Is there a conflict, in a student's perception, that a draft needs to be perfect to get a good grade? How can we help students to master a skill that depends almost entirely on them embracing the imperfection of creation? How can we demonstrate this paradox to our students?

5–7

How to Use the Fear of the Blank Page to Fuel Your Writing

Most likely, I will never write without procrastinating, without being a little blocked, without feeling the perfectionistic itch. I understand these postures as a defense against the tiger in the tall grass. I see you, saboteur, lurking in my brain, but I'm going to channel you into some radical creative energy on the page.

My goal is to help students see anxiety, not as an indication they're flawed, but as a sign they've entered into the creative realm. To ask students to drag these conditions out into the open, name them, and dismantle their power and lessen their destructiveness to write. To give students strategies to mitigate the anxiety and reframe the fear. To give students a growing storeroom of positive writing experiences.

Students who anticipate their writing anxiety and understand how to use coping strategies feel more in control of their situation, thereby better equipped to cope and overcome. I use the following six strategies nearly every week in my classroom and in my life as a writer to reposition positive anxiety in the service of work.

Talk About It

As a classroom teacher, the single best thing I can do for writers who deal with writing anxiety is to talk about it, share our stories, and ask other students to share theirs. Normalizing and naming the fear is a behavioral strategy called "affect labeling" used not only to quiet the inflamed fight-flight-or-freeze limbic system, but to allow a community of writers to grow, building trust and empathy with each other through their stories (Lieberman et al. 2007). Expressing how the anxiety feels can help a student understand not only her emotions, but her maladaptive thoughts around the act of writing as well. Hearing others share their story confirms and reinforces that anxiety is a normal, even essential, part of the process.

Talking and sharing your thoughts with others is also a way to recognize and amend distorted thinking (i.e., "I failed a writing assignment when I was in middle school, so I will always be a failure at writing"). If a student experiences anxiety around writing and hears a dozen stories of the same from her peers and her teacher, her own emotional reaction comes more into perspective. It's not the beastie in the grass, just a garden variety writing assignment.

Teaching Strategy for a Small Class

Write the words *writer's block*, *procrastination*, and *perfectionism* on pieces of butcher paper and hang these around the room. Ask students to participate in a silent dialogue (sometimes called the Big Paper on the Wall strategy) with the words. They can write what these words remind them of or their experiences with these conditions or how these conditions make them feel. After everyone has participated, ask anyone if they'd like to share a story about dealing with these issues. After the class has had sufficient time to share, turn the Big Papers over and ask students to brainstorm coping strategies they may have used in the past to overcome blank page anxiety. Once everyone has participated, discuss the strategies. Have students vote on the five most effective strategies from the list. Copy those on an anchor chart to use for the rest of the year. An extension for this activity would be to create a smaller eight-and-a-half-by-eleven-inch chart of effective coping strategies for each condition to be typed up and laminated for future individual intervention.

Teaching Strategy for a Larger Class
Hand out Figure 5–1 (front of the handout) and give writers time to fill in their experiences, stories, and feelings around these three writing anxieties. After they've written, ask two or three to share a story or an experience. After sharing, ask students to flip the handout over (Figure 5–2) and brainstorm effective coping strategies they have used in the past or would like to try out.

Breathe Through It

Breathing seems like a simple solution to a complex problem, but in 2010, two hundred Aetna employees who participated in deep breathing exercises through yoga and meditation classes provided by their company for three months reported less stress and better sleep. After using these exercises that regulate the breath, the employees even reported decreased health care costs. In a follow-up study, researchers discovered not only were the employees less stressed and sleeping better, but experienced "47 to 62 minutes of increased productivity per week" (Jabr 2020, 82).

One of the easiest ways to control stress is to control your breathing. Andrew Huberman, a Stanford University neuroscientist, explains why: "Our lungs consist of tons of tiny little sacs of air—millions of sacs of air. As we get stressed, these little sacs collapse. They deflate like a balloon" (Wapner 2020, 58). Huberman says deep breathing directly impacts the stress response and brings "the level of autonomic arousal back down to baseline." By filling the lungs with air and moving the diaphragm up and down, the heart expands and slows, blood flow slows, and we become calmer. Focusing on the inhale/exhale pattern of the breathing allows us to concentrate on something other than our fear.

To aid students in developing a breathing practice around writing, I model this in front of the class. Sometimes I ask our physical education teacher to lead us in a breath exercise, and sometimes I do it myself, but the setup is easy.

Ask students to push away from their desk and sit comfortably in their chair, and think of a writing assignment that gives them anxiety. Here's the script I use: "With your eyes closed, visualize yourself writing. When anxiety rises up in the

Figure 5–1 ∼ *What Is Blank Page Anxiety?*

All writers have experienced these three conditions at some point when faced with the blank page. Have you or anyone you know experienced these conditions? How did it feel? What was your experience? What story could you tell about how this anxiety felt? Jot down a description of what each feels like to you or an experience you've had with these states of mind.		
Writer's Block	**Procrastination**	**Perfectionism**

Figure 5–2 ~ *What Are Coping Strategies for Blank Page Anxiety?*

All writers have had to develop strategies to write with these fears. What are some of the strategies you or someone you know has tried in the past? What is an effective activity or intervention or technique that will help a writer overcome blank page anxiety? List three to five strategies to help someone struggling with getting started on a writing assignment.

Writer's Block	Procrastination	Perfectionism

pit of your stomach, breathe slowly in and out. Begin by counting your breath. One, inhale; two, exhale; three, inhale; four exhale, and so on, until you feel yourself calming down. Again, try to visualize yourself starting to write. Does the image conjure fear? Resume the breathing practice until the visualization of starting to write does not fill you with dread."

Script for Leading Students in a Relaxed Breathing

Sit up in your chair with both feet planted on the floor. Lay your hands comfortably in your lap. Close your eyes. Slowly breath in through your nose for four counts. Hold it for four counts, then, in four counts, slowly release the breath. Take in another inhale for four counts. Hold it for four counts, then release. Take in another deep inhale. Hold it for four counts, then release. Scan your body for any tightness or nervousness. Breath in deeply for four counts, and when you exhale, relax the part of your body—your neck, your back, your shoulders, your temples—that feels the tension. Repeat as many times as necessary to feel relaxed.

Move with It

Although you probably can't dismiss class and take your students on a nice long jog to get their blood pumping, movement is another way to calm anxiety around the act of writing. Encourage students, if they are at home and the words just aren't flowing, to walk, run, skip, or hop around the block a couple of times and let the off-task part of their brain begin the process of solving the problem of the writing. In class, put on some music and invite students to dance, shake, or jump in place to release tension, increase oxygen intake, and stimulate their brains.

Walking is especially helpful when you're agitated and can't settle down to write. Use the motion to connect with the present moment, paying attention to your breath, your hands as they swing by your side, your feet as they touch the ground, the sounds and smells around you. The movement will loosen the tension you hold in your body and may inspire you with ideas if you are blocked. The pace and the intensity don't have to set Olympic goals, just a good old British stroll will do. (For a delightful book about the stimulating benefits of writers walking, check out Duncan Minshull's [2019] *Beneath My Feet: Writers on Walking*, which gathers the stories of thirty-six different writers from Petrarch to Nietzsche who benefitted from the practice.)

Stretching Activity, Seated to Standing
Push your chair away from your desk. Reach your hands up to the ceiling. Take a deep breath and stand up. Hinge forward from your hips, collapsing over your stomach, and hang like a rag doll. Take another deep breath. Cross your arms over and let them hang heavy. Take another deep breath. Feel all the stress melt out of your back and the backs of your legs. Slowly reach down and touch your shins, your ankle, your toes, or the floor. Take another deep breath, then slowly curl back up to standing position.

Stretching the Head and Neck
Drop your right ear to your right shoulder. Feel the stretch along the left side of your neck. Breathe in deeply for four counts, hold, then exhale slowly. Drop your left ear to your left shoulder. Feel the stretch along the right side of your neck. Breathe in deeply for four counts, hold, then exhale slowly. Repeat both sides four times to relax the tension in the head and neck.

Write About It

Research shows that recognizing the source of one's anxiety and addressing it, rather than ignoring it or burying it, is critical. Dr. Ron Siegel (2010) writes in *The Mindfulness Solution*, "Approaching what we fear and staying with it until the anxiety eventually abates works for almost all anxiety problems. It is the opposite of escape-avoidance learning and is a path toward psychological freedom" (81).

One way to overcome the fear of writing is to write about it, which fulfills three goals: (1) writing helps create mindfulness around the fear, (2) writing about the fear allows students to practice writing, which creates fluency, and (3) writing about the fear lessens the severity or dissipates the fear entirely.

Write with the Fear

Sometimes when students are stuck on the blank page, I ask them to interrogate and explore the fear first: *Why am I scared to write this? Why am I scared of getting started? Why does this writing task intimidate me?*

The act of writing winds up their gears. Writing about fear helps address, express, and ultimately relieve the tension students feel. Writing was the goal all along, and writing about the fear is a way to approach the fear, as Siegel suggests, and stay with it. Here is a strategy I model for my students:

Writing with Fear Strategy

- Set a timer for five minutes. Write for the whole time just describing the physical anxiety you feel. How does the fear express itself in your inner thoughts? How does the fear express itself in your body? Your breathing? Your neck and shoulders?

  » Take a break. Stretch. Walk around, get a drink of water.

- Return to your desk and set the timer again for five minutes. This time, write *about* the project you are supposed to be writing about. Don't write the project or assignment or task you're supposed to be writing: write about it. What thoughts do you have about this assignment? Do you hate it? Say that. Get it all on the page. Write about how much you hate it or how much you love it or how much you love or hate the teacher (or the boss or professor) who has given you this task.

  » Take a break. Stretch. Walk around, get a drink of water.

- Return to your desk and set the timer again for five minutes This time, begin writing the assignment. If you find yourself blocked or stuck, start the process all over again. Write about the fear. Write about the assignment. Then start on the assignment. All in five-minute increments.

Write Forward, Don't Delete

One day last semester, I got a frantic email from one of my ninth-grade writers. "I don't know what I'm doing! Help!" As we were virtually doing school those days, we jumped online and talked it through. She had written four hundred words, then thought it was awful and deleted the whole thing. Then she wrote another eight hundred words and thought that was awful and was on the verge of deleting that as well. I assured her what she was doing was a normal, yet ultimately demoralizing practice with most writers.

"Why are you deleting these drafts?" I asked.

"Because they're horrible!" She was near tears. "They sounded like a third grader wrote them."

I suggested she not delete her work anymore, but take a break from it, come back the next day, and read it with fresh eyes.

"Do you think you might struggle with perfectionism?" I asked. She said yes, she knew that was part of the problem.

"Have you heard the phrase, 'perfect is the enemy of the good'?"

"My mom says that to me all the time," she said, laughing. "She tells me done is better than perfect."

I was still thinking about our Zoom meeting when I met with some seniors who were working on college essays, one of the most anxiety-producing writing tasks of their young lives. I told them about my freshman student, and I asked them how they might have advised her. Elke's response was so smart I'm including it here:

> I empathize with this writer because I, too, am a perfectionist and I, too, hate everything I write. I've come to learn "done is better than perfect." If she keeps deleting everything she writes, she will be too busy deleting to ever write anything worth keeping. Maybe what she wrote wasn't good, but if she kept writing, she would likely stumble upon something better, and better, and better. She could also pick the best line from what she had already written and build off of that. Or, she could write the antithesis of what she'd already written. The important thing for her to do is to write forward, instead of writing in circles. Write through the bad. She could also find an activity that helps her think through things, away from the page. For me, it's when I drive, lay in bed (without falling asleep), or take a shower. In those settings, I can work everything out. She can find the equivalent for herself and come back to the page the next day.

I love Elke's suggestion to "write forward" and "write through the bad." To students who are having a tough time getting started, I remind them of the five-minute practice. Set a timer for five minutes and tell yourself: all I have to do is write for five minutes. To students who are really having a hard time, I might amend the five-minute practice to the one sentence practice: just write one sentence. That's it. Just get one sentence on the page. That's all you have to do.

Write Like Nobody's Reading

Every year, my freshman writing class does the National Novel Writing Month (NaNoWriMo) challenge. They pledge to write fifty thousand words of a novel in thirty days. The challenge produces something worth more than a book contract: a knowledge of one's own limits and an answer to the lie that fear tells you. Students tell themselves they can't do it, but this experience always teaches them they can.

The goal then becomes not necessarily to write a novel, but to give yourself permission to write as badly as you want to write to push yourself to see if you can do it. I know there are people reading who will be horrified by this, that this kind of recklessness will lead to poor writing habits, but I've never seen any evidence that more writing leads to less fluency in the craft. (For more great wisdom, check out Grant Faulkner's [2017] book *Pep Talks for Writers: 52 Insights and Actions to Boost Your Creative Mojo.*)

My peer tutor Emma took the NaNoWriMo challenge as a freshman and now she was helping my ninth graders with their novels. She wrote: "When I did NaNoWriMo, the more I wrote the more in control of the story I felt like I was. I grew closer to the characters, and it felt as if I could just easily type out their journeys. The gaps that I had left I went back and filled in with more confidence. My advice would be to stop worrying about perfection. I know, blah, that's some of the most common advice that you can get, and it's the hardest to follow. But it's also completely worth it—I wholeheartedly believe in that."

Another student, Sydney, wrote of the experience: "I wrote like nobody would see it. I just wrote as much as I could. If I didn't know where I was going with a particular plotline, I would switch it up. If I didn't want to write a scene or felt like I didn't want to write it at the moment, I would skip it. If I felt like I wrote myself into a corner, I'd turn and leave the room, and write a different part of the story. And in the end, I had about 50,000 words of a rough draft—and I actually loved it."

The goal is to write less for the finished product and more to learn of the journey and to learn about your own writing habits. Give yourself permission to write badly and the awareness that revision is where writing is born.

Make a Plan

Making a physical plan before you write is a great way to mitigate the fear of the blank page. Sketching out even the most rudimentary plan allows students time to ruminate about how an essay might look and sound. In Robert Caro's (2019) memoir on research and writing, *Working,* he describes his planning process:

> I can't start a book until I've thought it through and can see it whole in my mind. So before I start writing, I boil the book down to three paragraphs, or two, or one—that's when it comes into view. When you have it, it's so comforting, because you're typing away, and you can look over—it's stuck to the wall right there. (196)

Many of my students find writing an outline as a necessary first step to both quell the fear of getting started and getting started at the same time. Using an outline often helps students see the relationship between ideas around a specific topic before they get lost in the weeds of the subject itself. Offering students multiple planning options gives the planners in your room some peace.

Planning Options for Writers

- Make a list of ideas around a specific topic. Rearrange the ideas into an outline that shows the relationships between them.

- Map out the relationships between these ideas. Make several maps if necessary using these patterns: similarity/comparison, opposite/contrast, time/chronological, cause/effect, reason/result, addition/subtraction, exampling/illustrating/exemplifying.

- Cluster ideas in a narrative pattern. Change the clusters to show patterns of storytelling, starting with beginning, middle, and end or Act I, Act II, and Act III.

- Diagram ideas into smaller components. (Example: "Dogs" becomes "small dogs" becomes "corgis" becomes "Pembroke Welsh corgis" becomes "Queen Elizabeth's Pembroke Welsh corgis.") Analyze the components for smaller or smaller parts. Rearrange these components into an outline.

- Freewrite about an idea, then highlight the main points. Extract the main points and arrange those in an outline. Then freewrite again from the outline.

- Draft a paragraph, then rearrange the sentences into a different pattern. Repeat four times, rearranging the sentences in different combinations each time. Consider how the different paragraph arrangements show different relationships between the ideas. (You can do this with an entire essay as well, but it's best to model this technique for your students using a small, manageable paragraph with about six to eight sentences.)

- Journal about an idea asking yourself the old journalistic standby five Ws and one H: write out the who, what, where, when, why, and how of a topic. Make an outline that represents each component.

Create a Ritual, Form a Habit

In *The Power of Habit*, Charles Duhigg (2012) examines the power of routine as a way to develop good habits and supplant bad ones. He examines the neurological loop discovered by MIT researchers that reveals the circuit that results in habit forming. The loop has three parts: a cue, a routine, and a reward. Some of my students naturally and unconsciously do this: the classroom bell cues them to begin work; they have a routine that includes checking their agenda, pulling out their Chromebooks, and writing. This behavior unlocks the reward they want: meeting their writing goals.

Students who struggle with creating a productive habit may need to intentionally arrange a cue (after I've fixed myself a cup of coffee) to launch into a routine (I'm going to write for twenty minutes on my essay) to reap a reward (if I write for twenty minutes, I'm going to reward myself with five minutes in Instagram). This habit circuit can be problematic in that, as a teacher, I want the reward of writing to be the writing itself. Also students may hack the circuit and go directly to the reward, thereby by doubling down on the distractions. But showing students this pattern of forming a habit does help them become conscious of the power of repeated behavior to achieve goals.

If you don't have a writing ritual, think about two or three personal cues you could use to prepare your mind to write. My work is produced in ten- to fifteen-minute bursts, sometimes while in a meeting. In those kinds of writes, there are few rituals, other than being struck by an idea and jotting it down in my iPhone notes. But when I go into my office with a hot cup of tea, shut the door, and light a candle, I've completed a ritual that signals to my mind: we are writing.

In 2014, behavior researcher Katherine Milkman and her colleagues coined the term "temptation bundling" as another way to reward yourself by indulging in a temptation only after you've completed a necessary task. This strategy works by "bundling" an action you need to do (exercise, writing, cleaning, and so on) with an action you want to do (watching a movie, reading a book, listening to a podcast).

Both habit loops and temptation bundling use rewards for behavior that generates productive habits. Understand that sitting down at the computer is the first step, and congratulate yourself for just doing that. Sandwich twenty minutes of writing between ten minutes of watching YouTube and ten minutes of texting a friend. Instead of giving yourself a star only when you have finished the large project at the end of the semester, why not give yourself a star for showing up every day you didn't avoid writing?

Of course, all these habit strategies require maturity, self-regulation, and investment in the task at hand, but sharing these with students at least gives them a few ideas of how to eat the elephant of a major writing assignment. And according to novelist Octavia Butler (1995), habit even exceeds inspiration for getting started. "First forget inspiration. Habit is more dependable. Habit will sustain you whether you're inspired or not. Habit will help you finish and polish your stories. Inspiration won't. Habit is persistence in practice" (141).

Fear of
Being Exposed

When I was in graduate school, I wrote a short story based on a trip I took from Cincinnati to San Francisco on a Greyhound bus. In the short story, an older Black female character tells the fifteen-year-old white female protagonist a vital piece of wisdom that protects her from being exploited by a predator on the bus.

As we workshopped the story, one of my friends remarked, "The next time you feel the need to write that tired old racist chestnut, let me know, so I can bitch-slap you into next week."

I was mortified. "What?"

He laughed.

"I didn't mean it that way," I said.

"Of course you didn't." He rolled his eyes.

I appreciated the comment, but I was embarrassed as well. Embarrassed I had written something so obvious to everyone else that had escaped me. I felt shame: my face turned red, my breathing quickened, and I wanted to crawl into a hole. I hadn't read widely enough or thought deeply enough. I had written something that exposed me, at best a feckless rube, at worst, a racist.

All writers feel this fear. Or some similar fear—of making fools of ourselves, saying something erroneously that doesn't align with our values. For professional writers, the fear of being exposed as a hack prompts exhaustive fact checking, regulating one's voice, refining the tone. These practices are ethical, necessary, and part of the writing profession. But for beginning writers, the fear is more existential. Not that you might have written something incorrect or racist or dunderheaded, but that you *are* incorrect, racist, and dunderheaded. By getting the writing wrong, you are exposing yourself as the wrong kind of person, whatever that is.

With my students, a host of fears circle around this idea of exposure. If I write something and don't get it right, my teacher will think I'm dumb, or I will get a bad grade. If I write something about my family, I might be taken away from them. What would my grandmother think if she read this? What would my priest say if he knew I didn't believe in God?

Think about how grave this threat of exposure is for students whose home language is different from their school language, those who experience body and voice dysmorphia or those who just don't understand how school works. A student may think, *If I say something and want to take it all back, I can deny I've said it, but if I write it down, it is there, in black and white. And what if I get it wrong because I don't know how to express myself, and people misunderstand me, and I cause trouble for my family or myself? I can't take that chance.*

Even my mother, an intelligent, college-educated woman, had the idea that writing was a window into the soul you might not want open. One day as I scribbled away in my journal, she warned, "If you keep writing things down like that, someone's going to read it." Her threat was clear. Writing exposes you in a way you don't want to be exposed.

As cynical as my mother's view was, she's not out of line with what many parents may perceive about a writing teacher's unique insight into their child's life through writing. I've lost count of the number of parents who wistfully (and low-key suspiciously) look at me as if I hold the magical key to understanding their distant teen: "She never lets me read what she writes in your class." There's an alienating element between school and home already, and writing is an activity wherein students bring that home culture to bear, writing from their experience.

Writing poses this risk: the writer unintentionally exposes herself to ridicule, rejection, and possibly punishment. Even among professional writers, who understand the necessity of research and self-awareness and technical craft, the nagging fear that the reader will be able to divine something deeply personal between the black-and-white words is always there. It is the fear that readers will read between the lines and understand something about you that you didn't know about yourself.

What Is It?

The blindness that plagues a writer—writing about one thing, revealing another—is the paradoxical purpose of why we write, to discover something that was hidden. Writing about something you cannot see clearly will give you insight and revelation. This awareness is one of the very purposes of writing. But self-awareness can be a powder keg of shame.

Writing dances between exploring the hidden and declaring a truth. All of us who write know what we write today may not be what we believe tomorrow, that the frozen record of a writer's evolution contains both the horrors and joys of pursuing the writing life. But for students who have not measured the risks against the joys, the disclosure of a secret revealed through writing may shut them down.

Professional writers, journalists, and memoirists write despite the danger their writing might deliver. The scientist who publishes research that challenges a powerful industry, a journalist exposing the crimes of a despot, a memoirist who reveals exploitation despite the social costs: all examples of pen wielding that comes with dangerous consequences for the writer. Although my students' writing may not topple autocratic governments, the fear of being exposed or being punished as a consequence of writing is just as real.

The statistics about bullying are well known. According to their annual survey of teen behavior, the Centers for Disease Control reports nearly a fifth of high school students are bullied in school, and 14.9 percent have experienced cyberbullying (DeSilver 2019). Female students and students who identify as LGBTQIA+ are even more likely to be victims of harassment. The resistance to a writing assignment, then, may not be laziness or technical ignorance, but self-protection.

One of my cardinal classroom rules is this: what's written in room 303 stays in room 303, unless the writer chooses to publish it. This is not an antitransparency policy, but as a protection for each writer in the room. Of course, if a student expresses a desire to hurt himself or others, I am bound by law to report this, and I have done that twice in my twenty-five-year career. But barring an alert-level piece, what students write is safe within this community. I don't share work, including with parents and counselors, unless I ask the writer first.

The potential for embarrassment presents a number of hurtles for the beginning writer to overcome. And yet, with each assignment, writing teachers ask students to take some portion of their inner lives and trot them out in a few paragraphs. Even though this practice is valuable and essential—research shows there are psychological and physical benefits to writing about memories (Pennebaker 2004)—it is no less intimidating. To externalize what students have buried and protected is terrifying territory indeed.

> Does writing about your life make you feel uncomfortable or excited? Does argumentative or analytical writing feel "safer" than personal or expressive writing? Why or why not?

6-1

> Has the fear of embarrassment ever stopped you or stifled you from writing something? Were you able to overcome your embarrassment and continue writing or did you avoid the task altogether? What happened?

6-2

> Think back over your writing life—as an elementary school student, as a high school student, as an undergraduate or a graduate student. Can you remember a writing assignment in which you discovered something about yourself? What are some revelations you made about yourself through writing?

6-1

> Can you remember any writing assignment that asked you to step outside of your comfort zone? How did this assignment make you feel? Were you able to write despite those feelings? If so, how did you overcome the fear of exposure? If not, what happened?

6-2

How Does It Feel?

Both a liberating and alienating experience, education asks students to unearth their values and beliefs and examine them. Part of that examination includes analyzing one's own neighborhood, family, and self. Writing, then, is a kind of soil sampling we ask students to make in the name of education. To drop a sampling plug down into the strata of our personal codes and traditions. Then analyze the findings and articulate it all in a smooth style. Done right, writing is a protracted, invasive process, one that exhumes and discloses the elements of our self that are the most personal—our value system, our beliefs, our memories.

Writing may feel like a betrayal of the people we love. Yet bringing students, whose ideas put them on the margins of society, into the mainstream with nonthreatening conversations and reflections is the most important part of our job as teachers. It's not, however, without risk for both students and teachers.

If students associate shame with their background or identity, they may be ill positioned to take the assured stances writers must take. Students who live in repressive, unquestioning places—in prejudiced homes, in isolated and homogeneous neighborhoods, in toxic religious sects—are the very students who would most benefit from the introspective force of writing, yet are the most vulnerable to its dangers.

Perhaps you do not assign writing assignments that ask students to dip into their personal experiences. The risk is there nonetheless. All writing—regardless of the genre, form, or purpose—is personal because it is processed through and by a person. When teachers ask students to pick an opinion and defend it, some risk is present, either from choosing an unpopular or illogical position or from being unable to mount the necessary defense. Students feel nervous about staking a claim, even if they fervently believe in it. Students may think: *What if someone challenges the way I think? What if my writing puts me at odds with my friends?*

Writing can feel like a performative code-switch. As a child of a strict fundamentalist family, I often left the house wearing one set of clothes and changed into another set for school. This kind of sartorial assimilation was necessary to maintain peace at home while also exploring another kind of person I wanted to become. Writing can be that exploratory outlet for students, but it's not without hazards.

A few months before Marlon James was awarded the Booker Prize for *A Brief History of Seven Killings*, he published the essay, "From Jamaica to Minnesota to Myself" (2015), in which he chronicled his journey as a gay, black writer who grew up in a hypermasculine, fundamentalist household. "When you're in a Jamaican or African or Arab closet—you love your parents, but in some ways you feel like you can't be free until they die." For students who live in one world and exist in another, writing can be a welcome release, a safe space, but it can also be a mother who finds an essay and uses it to shut down a transformation.

Even writing fiction can be a painful risk and a powerful release. Marlon (2015) writes that "characters arise out of our need for them." Students who write a character who is violent and racist to make sense of their own violent and racist life may feel the social costs of giving that work to a group of friends. Paradoxically, there is a powerful release in writing representative characters and giving them voice, finally, on the block for all to see.

For anyone who has ever taught literature to high school students, you can teach persona as a literary element all day long and preach about how a reader should distance the character from the writer himself, yet students invariably conflate the two. Writing creates enough tissue between the person who is writing and the person he is writing about to create a fear of exposure, especially for a novice writer who may not feel in control of technique. When students who write fiction in my class submit writing for feedback, they almost always contextualize their submission with some reiteration of "Oh by the way, this isn't me."

As an adult, I've been in writing workshops, retreats, and classes where the expectation to share our work is part of the contract of the class. Vulnerability is absolutely necessary, yet can be threatening to the novice writer.

> How does it feel to share personal writing with other students in your class? Do you feel comfortable sharing your writing or do you feel your peers will judge you, instead of just offering feedback on your writing? Why or why not?

6-3

> In an interview with *The Paris Review*, Salman Rushdie (Gourevitch 2008) said, ". . . if you write about everywhere you can end up writing about nowhere. It's a problem that a writer writing about a single place does not have to face" (361). What does Rushdie mean when he says that writing about everywhere ends up as writing about nowhere? Where is the single place, either geographically or emotionally, from which you write? Do you feel comfortable writing about your family, your community, your neighborhood?

6-4

6-3

In "Dangerous Writing," an essay on the dangers and joys of exposure as a writer, novelist Tom Spanbauer writes, "As a child, raised Catholic, I was to be seen and not heard, and I was beaten any time I expressed myself. I was told never to show off. To never make a spectacle of myself. And here I am in front of you" (2016, 37). How can you, as a writing teacher, mitigate the embarrassment that students might feel while writing, while also encouraging students to take risks when choosing writing topics? How can you encourage the best work while helping the writer navigate potential ridicule and bullying?

6-4

Examine two writing assignments you normally give your students. What fears of exposure might these assignments present to your students? What brainstorming or community-building exercises might benefit students who are fearful of an assignment that requires them to write about a deeply held belief or a valued tradition? How might you acknowledge or prepare them?

How Does It Manifest in Writers?

Every malady that shows up in writers who have blank page anxiety—writer's block, perfectionism, and procrastination—also shows up in writers who fear exposure, but there are a few particular ills that seem to beset writers who are highly susceptible to shame. In *The Gifts of Imperfection*, Brown (2010) outlines the defenses humans use when faced with shame: "Some of us *move away* by withdrawing, hiding, silencing ourselves, and keeping secrets. Some of us *move toward* by seeking to appease and please. And some of us *move against* by trying to gain power over others, by being aggressive" (46). These stances—moving away, moving toward, and moving against—are at the heart of the three responses that novice writers exhibit when faced with the fear of exposure and shame from something they've written.

   For the purposes of illustration, let's take a sample writing assignment and run it through these three fear postures, considering how a fictional student might be wary of writing an essay that presents a risk to his self-concept or social capital. Here's a typical school writing assignment: "Write a two- to four-page (500–1,000 words) argumentative essay about a controversial topic that exists in contemporary society."

This assignment is multipurposed: it invites students to step into contemporary discourse; to engage in critical thinking, research, logic, and rhetorical arrangement; and to examine their own thinking, prejudices, values, and beliefs.

Self-Protection: Moving Away

Students who come from homes where performance is emphasized and conformity is prized tend to choose safe writing topics that require little emotional risk. This choice protects them from potential punishment from family or friends. The writing doesn't challenge them, but neither does it expose them.

Let's say Tejah is a politically active junior in a midsize urban school in Georgia. She is inspired by an upcoming election to volunteer for several voter registration drives, and she becomes active in a political science club at school. When her Advanced Placement language arts teacher assigns our sample assignment, Tejah's immediate thought is to write about gerrymandering, something she doesn't know much about, but that she's vitally interested in.

After researching, Tejah begins to write, but she throws away her first three introductory paragraphs because they sound dumb and childish. She can't get all the research to come together. She's not sure what she thinks or wants to say about gerrymandering. Tejah's parents are constantly pressuring her to keep her grade point average up, so she can get into a good college. If she writes about gerrymandering, it might be personally more satisfying, but it would take a lot of work, and the essay might not score well. She finally decides to take an essay she wrote about gun control as a freshman and revise it. There's no real risk of failure, and there's less work.

Faced with our sample assignment, Jesus, whose father is an undocumented worker, could write about immigration. This subject is vital to his life, a subject that could be both intellectually stimulating and emotionally beneficial. But the subject is also risky because it might endanger someone he loves if he uses his own experience. He then chooses to write his argumentative essay on cell phone use in the classroom, an essay he may care little about, but is safe and easily written.

There's nothing wrong with either Tejah's or Jesus' decision to defer a risky subject for a safer one. Rejecting a topic or assessing the emotional labor to produce a piece of writing is part of a student's developing self-regulation. Professional writers make these decisions daily about what they write and the constraints and boundaries of their writing life. Both Tejah's and Jesus' choice also meant they didn't have to research as much and could spend more time on writing, revising, and drafting, another mature decision for a growing writer.

However, if the community of writers exists in a safe, sharing environment and the exploration of personally significant topics is supported, students will feel more comfortable to embrace a topic that requires discomfort, but pays out emotional growth and writing maturity. Also, if the grading system in place allows for students to learn from the failure inherent in writing while not failing the assignment or failing the class, students will take risks with their writing.

6-5   Do you prefer writing assignments that allow you to choose your own topic or do you like writing assignments that provide you with a topic? When faced with a choose-your-own-topic assignment, do you tend to choose a safe topic or one that challenges you? Why or why not?

6-5   Many writing assignments require little more than reading some research and writing up a summary of it. Yet even when teachers craft assignments that center a student's experience or that allow students to choose their own topics, a student could still "move away" from a challenging topic and choose a topic that is safe and easy. Consider the writing assignments you give in your classroom. Do you offer both self-selected and teacher-assigned topics? Which of these paths offers students more agency and autonomy?

Teacher Pleasing: Move Toward

Although some students may move away from a topic that threatens to expose a personal insecurity, other students may move toward an assignment from a need to fawn or perform for praise. If they feel shame around the act of writing or don't respect their own ideas, they may seek to please the teacher and fortify themselves against the shame of appearing deficient as a writer. Instead of engaging in a writing assignment that might lead to self-discovery, students with a high shame response may respond by writing about a teacher's pet topic. *What does the teacher want or like? If the teacher wants or likes X, I will give them X.*

When faced with our example writing assignment, Jamal wants to write about racism and how the school he attends has numerous racist practices and policies that need to be addressed. However, Jamal may feel shame surrounding this topic or feel that his grade or his position within the classroom may be poisoned. His teacher doesn't talk about race, and he feels if he does, he may be targeted as a troublemaker.

Amy has a strong pro-life stance, but she knows, or suspects, that her teacher is pro-choice. She may choose to write about another topic because she needs a good grade in this class and doesn't believe that her teacher will be able to separate her own personal beliefs from her job as a teacher.

Of course, students who aren't threatened by writing assignments at all might write to teacher-please merely as a way to garner a good grade. They might also choose a topic that won't challenge their beliefs or reveal inconsistencies to be examined, but students who are highly compliant and prone to people-pleasing to get approval will shy away from subjects in an effort to avoid the risk.

> Have you ever chosen to write about a topic because you knew your teacher would like the subject? Did this feel like you were cheating yourself or was it necessary to just get through the class? Why do you think students choose to write about topics they know their teacher will like? *6-6*

> When students choose to write from an argumentative position you disagree with, how do you mitigate your personal response and reach out to help them shore up their arguments? *6-6*

Anger: Moving Against

Students may perceive a writing prompt as a trick to reveal a part of themselves they wish to keep private. Students may respond in anger when an assignment touches on these soft spots. The anger might be directed at the teacher, school in general, or just a free-floating dissatisfaction that presents itself as defiance. Anger may also evolve into procrastination as a way of dealing with an assignment they feel threatened by. There are a host of reasons why students don't complete assignments, but students who feel shame around the emotional labor of writing may react aggressively or passive-aggressively to remove themselves from it.

Khrystyl's teacher has assigned our sample writing assignment, but Khrystyl doesn't feel she knows enough to write about anything successfully. Maybe she doesn't understand the assignment or feels like any topic she would select wouldn't be "good enough" to write a whole essay about. She feels like the other kids in the room are smarter than she is, and if she attempts to write anything, it will expose her lack of knowledge and lack of skill. So she doesn't do the assignment. This causes her teacher to reach out to her, ask questions, offer help. Perhaps her grandmother calls the school to get more information about the missing assignment. Perhaps Khrystyl gets into trouble. She feels the need to protect herself, so she may even develop a narrative that the teacher is out to get her, that school is stupid, that the assignment was dumb. This anger response more easily assuages the fear of exposure. Anger is easier than attempting the assignment and being faced with the consequences of her own shame.

6-7 Have you ever felt that a writing assignment was an intrusion into your personal life? How did you react? Could you have discussed this with your teacher and advocated for a different assignment? Why or why not?

6-7 Can you remember a student who has responded in anger to a particular writing assignment? What was the source of the anger? How could you have resolved it or attempted to resolve it?

How to Use Fear of Being Exposed to Fuel Your Writing

In his book *Writing to Heal*, psychologist James Pennebaker (2004) describes his research related to expressive writing and trauma in the late '80s. In four different studies, he recruited University of Texas–Austin students who knew they would be required to write for fifteen minutes a day for four consecutive days, but they weren't told what they would be writing about. When they arrived for the study, half were instructed to write about a traumatic event in their life, and the other half were given benign, nonemotional topics.

Pennebaker later called his original study "horribly underpowered," but the study revealed that students who wrote about trauma "ended up going to the student health center over the next six months at about half the rate of students in the control condition" (18). Pennebaker and his colleagues followed up this initial study with sixty-three professionals who'd been laid off from their jobs. In this study, participants wrote for thirty minutes for five consecutive days. One group was instructed to write about their feelings around the layoff, the control group was instructed to write about their plans for the day, and yet another group was given no writing instruction at all. After the study, the researchers followed each participant's employment status and discovered that those who wrote about their feelings around job loss were more likely to find employment in the eight months after the study (Spera, Buhrfeind, and Pennebaker 1994).

Secrecy fuels shame. A buried memory can haunt, but a memory expressed loses power quickly. I want to show students the cathartic gift writing has been for me. To express myself on the page, as a means of understanding myself, as a means of making sense of the world has been instrumental in my own emotional growth and intellectual clarity. My goal then is to name and normalize the shame, share my own struggles with it, and offer a few tips to deal with the fear of exposure. I use the following five strategies in my classroom to dismantle the power of shame from writing.

Talk About It

Demystify the shame all writers are prone to by talking it out. The anxiety of exposure is one that can be recognized, named, and examined to mitigate its disastrous effects. That nearly all writers feel this apprehension places student writers on equal footing with published authors of all ages, genders, and genres. Being judged by others is part of writing, and we create despite that.

Understanding that all writers feel this fear helps my students understand their fear is not unique. One way in which student writers can begin to dismantle the power of this fear is to understand how professional writers use their fear to bolster the energy of their work.

Teaching Strategy for a Small Class

On pieces of butcher paper around the room, write out the following quotes from Figure 6–1. Ask students to read the quotes and think about them. Then ask students to answer this question: "Do you agree or disagree with this statement? Why or why not?" Ask students to write their response on the corresponding butcher paper. After everyone has participated, ask anyone if they'd like to share a story about why they agreed or disagreed with what these professional writers describe.

Teaching Strategy for a Larger Class

Hand out Figure 6–1 and give writers time to read the quotes and think about them. Then ask students to answer these questions: Do you agree or disagree with this statement? Why or why not? Ask students to write their analysis on the cells below each quote on their handout. After everyone has participated, ask anyone if they'd like to share a story about why they agreed or disagreed with what these professional writers describe.

Reframe It

When we are startled or scared, our brain and body set in motion the physical postures to either fight or flee. But there is an emotional component too. For years, scientists thought our emotional response sparked our physiological response, but turns out, it's the other way around. Our brain sees the danger, floods the system with adrenaline, the body reacts, *then* we feel the fear. This means we can control our emotional response to stimuli.

For students who dread writing, this is good news. Fear or dread is just an interpretation of seeing a threat and feeling your heart race based on your past experiences. As students' writerly self-regard grows and they store more positive experiences with writing in their memory, their brain will use that information to interpret the task differently. In other words, they can reframe and control their emotional response.

Figure 6–1 ~ *Analyze the Fear of Being Embarrassed as a Writer*

Below are three professional writers musing about writers who feel shame around writing or creating. Read the quotes carefully, and analyze what the writers are saying. In the space below, answer the following question: Do you agree or disagree with this statement? Why or why not?		
"The moment that you feel that, just possibly, you're walking down the street naked, exposing too much of your heart and your mind and what exists on the inside, showing too much of yourself. That's the moment you may be starting to get it right." *Neil Gaiman said this during a 2012 commencement speech to graduates at the University of the Arts in Philadelphia who were pursuing jobs as artists in the world.*	"Write what disturbs you, what you fear, what you have not been willing to speak about. Be willing to be split open." *Natalie Goldberg (1986) wrote this in her book* Writing Down the Bones, *which helps people overcome their fear of writing failure.*	"Any writing exposes writers to judgment about the quality of their work and their thought. The closer they get to painful personal truths, the more fear mounts—not just about what they might reveal but about what they might discover should they venture too deeply inside. To write well, however, that's exactly where we must venture." *This is from* The Courage to Write, *a book Ralph Keyes (1995) wrote to help people overcome their fear of writing.*
Your Analysis:	**Your Analysis:**	**Your Analysis:**

By reframing the experience of writing as self-expression, as empowerment, as a puzzle, or as an opportunity to learn and grow, students may have an easier time writing. Channeling my inner creative child helps me. When I was a little, I wrote all kinds of stories and songs and poems. It was an ego's pure expression of itself for an audience of exactly one. The results didn't matter. I approached the writing with the joy of play, not the fear of embarrassment. What was I going to create? It had the potential to be anything. It might be the greatest thing ever to have been written.

Novelist Walter Mosley (2019) writes, "My advice when it comes to the first steps into emptiness, that moment when you embark on the self-revelation of the Word, my advice is that you approach it as a child would—that is, full of wonder and a sense of play. You have a keyboard and a blank screen, a pencil and a pristine piece of paper. These are the toys. Get used to them. Start putting down words" (7).

Reframe the fear. See the task differently. Keep throwing words out. Write from joy. Celebrate showing up.

Center Choice

Choice of topic, subject, mode, and purpose is one of the cornerstones of a healthy writing curriculum. Giving less prescriptive instructions and asking more questions allows students to gain control of their work (Figure 6–2). When students develop a psychological flexibility that helps them see writing as an opportunity for exploration instead of a rigid mandate designed to expose and belittle them, they begin to see writing not as a "gotcha" proposition, but an "I get you" possibility. Our job is to midwife their vision and help them make that cognitive and emotional shift.

Create Writing Boundaries

Talk early and often about emotional boundaries with students, especially students who might not recognize the dangers of oversharing, social exploitation, or bullying that comes from writing about something they're not ready to write about. Although telling a personal story honestly has an abundance of psychological benefits, students may not be mature enough to recognize their own emotional limits.

Figure 6–2 ~ *Ways to Center Choice in Writing*

Teachers	Students
• Provide students with dozens of no-stakes or low-stakes writing activities that generate topics and ideas.	• Consider a broad perspective rather than limiting yourself to one or two safe topics.
• Ask students what they are *trying* to write. Give them opportunities to draw, talk, or write about their writing ideas.	• Narrow down your topics to one or two ideas you are passionate about.
• Interrogate your own instructional practices that might supplant a student's writing aims with your learning targets.	• Look over a list of writing topics you've generated. Do you see patterns? Why are you drawn to certain topics?
• Create just as many real-world writing tasks without assigning form or purpose as you create tasks that come with an assigned form and purpose.	• Give yourself permission to feel a little scared when you are faced with a challenging writing assignment.
• Cultivate a supportive classroom environment where students feel safe and protected.	• Challenge your negative self-talk, by asking yourself: *Why does this assignment scare me?*
• Recognize some students want you to make a choice for them. Weigh the pros of assistance against the cons of dependency.	• Recognize anxiety for what it is, and think about the writing goals you've set for yourself.
	• Ask yourself: *How does this assignment challenge me to declare my truth?*
	• Ask yourself: *How can I approach this assignment as an opportunity for discovery and exploration?*

Part of growing as a writer is being able to understand the different stances one can take in front of an audience. Make it clear that choice is always a priority in writing, and certain subjects may be too embarrassing, thorny, or personal to share with the entire class. Those topics should be written about, but only in a private journal.

Three Levels of Writing Boundaries

- Only the writer sees private writing, best penned in a private journal or a diary. A writer can write about anything and everything in a diary because its total audience is an audience of one. If you choose, you may share something in your private diary or journal with a trusted family member, a friend, or your counselor or therapist.

- Semiprivate writing may be generated in a student's class writing notebook. The writing notebook is a semipublic record of their growth as a writer. Drafts of essays generated in the notebook may be shared with me or small inquiry groups. Also included in this category would be work with a limited distribution to a few trusted peers who are reading solely with the purpose of improving the writing, encouraging the writer, and fostering a better draft.

- Public writing is revised, edited, polished, and distributed to a wider audience, such as submitting the writing for a grade, to a schoolwide contest, to a public blog, or for publication online, in a magazine, or in a newspaper.

Among the first conversations I have with students is about the sanctity of one's own emotional territory, and although we, as writers, use that emotional territory to fuel our writing, students are not expected to open wide the gates of their interior life merely for a writing assignment. Students whose shame response is to teacher-please to get approval may unconsciously overshare in an effort to create a connection with the teacher. I intentionally teach the difference between private, semiprivate, and public writing. (See Figure 6–3.) One of the ways I demonstrate this is to encourage students to think about general boundaries around sharing their private lives.

Write About Fear in a Safe Space

Pennebaker's research, and several studies since then, demonstrate that writing about trauma, although initially painful and upsetting, can help the survivor in the long run. Writing about trauma is not the goal of the English language arts classroom, but using writing as a means to examine a stressful memory or event is a great assignment that helps student simultaneously practice writing, relieve stress, and write about their own lives. It also may unburden them of some shame surrounding certain memories or topics.

Figure 6–3 ~ *Creating Boundaries Around Writing Topics*

In the first two circles, name the people who are in the communication level on the right as audiences and brainstorm and write down possible topics on the left with the corresponding circle.

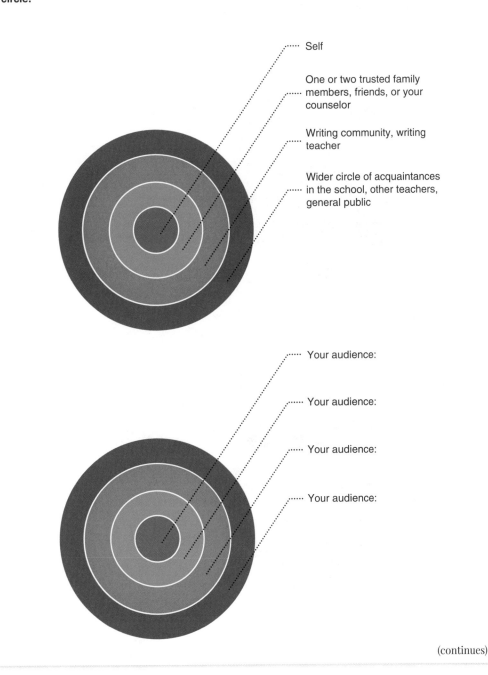

Self

One or two trusted family members, friends, or your counselor

Writing community, writing teacher

Wider circle of acquaintances in the school, other teachers, general public

Your audience:

Your audience:

Your audience:

Your audience:

(continues)

Figure 6–3 ~ *Creating Boundaries Around Writing Topics* (continued)

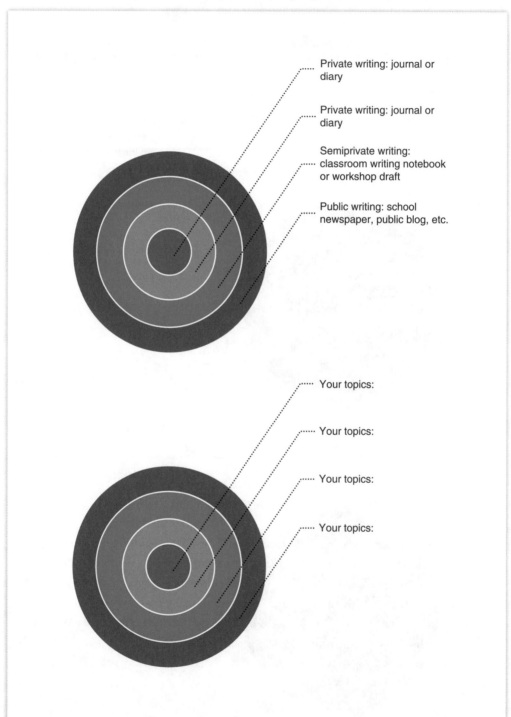

Private writing: journal or diary

Private writing: journal or diary

Semiprivate writing: classroom writing notebook or workshop draft

Public writing: school newspaper, public blog, etc.

Your topics:

Your topics:

Your topics:

Your topics:

Your topics:

Here are five writing prompts that help students write about personal topics without the expectation to share them.

Several years ago, Kentucky novelist Crystal Wilkinson came to my class to work with my writers and asked students to finish this sentence: "It would be much too dangerous to talk about . . ." It's one of the most successful writing prompts I use to get students to begin writing. Once we finish this writing prompt, I do not ask students to share their writing, but we do discuss the process and how it felt to write about a "dangerous" topic.

Another writing prompt that does a similar job I picked up from poet Jim Hall. At the beginning of his class, he asked us to write a letter to someone that we would never send. At the end of the class, he told us to shred the letters and throw them away. It was incredibly cathartic. Writing a letter to someone without the expectation to send it allows the writer to give voice to unexpressed anger without the social or emotional consequence.

Write in the third person, as if your topic were happening to someone else. Substitute *he*, *she*, or *they* for *I* and describe the experience from the third-person point of view. You can also write a blurb about the writing in third person, as if the piece has already been written. (This is a favorite NaNoWriMo trick: write a blurb for the dust jacket of your own book as if it were already written.) This is a powerful strategy called self-distancing, which is an "emotion-regulatory process that facilitates adaptive meaning-making" (Park, Ayduk, and Kross 2015, 1). Expressive writing has proven to be beneficial for both emotional and mental health, and psychologists believe that when people look at a negative experience from a self-distancing perspective, they can reflect, ruminate, and process the experience, "without becoming overwhelmed by negative emotional and physiological reactivity" (2).

Write a short note or a long letter to yourself as if you were writing to your best friend. Fill it with words of kindness, grace, and encouragement. Be frank and honest, telling yourself not to give up and not to be scared. Put the letter somewhere visible so that you can see it daily to remind you to persist and overcome.

Write an open letter to the voice inside your head. Writing a letter of protest is a great way to dismiss and banish the fear of being exposed by rejecting the very voice that threatens to embarrass you. Address it. Call it out. Put it on alert, and shut it down.

We Can Write Hard Things: Why Sharing the Struggle Is Powerful

In an interview with Studs Terkel (1989), James Baldwin spoke of the power of literature to create empathy and connection with other people. "You read something which you thought only happened to you, and you discover that it happened one hundred years ago to Dostoyevsky. This is a very great liberation for the suffering, struggling person, who always thinks that he is alone. This is why art is important. Art would not be important if life were not important, and life is important" (13).

Although students should be aware of the risks of sharing their story, they also should recognize how motivating and inspirational one person overcoming discomfort to tell their story can be. My student Marley wrote a blog about living with an abusive parent. She had tried to write about this before, but had always talked herself out of it from the fear of how others might view her. One day in workshop, a friend suggested she write it not so much for herself, but for other kids, younger kids, who might be living with an abusive parent.

Marley writes:

> So, I did. It was a very difficult first step, but once I'd created my reasoning for writing the blog in the first place, to help other

kids of abusive parents understand and overcome the challenges they face, the hurdle suddenly shrunk. I wasn't just writing about myself anymore; I was writing to help others like me who didn't know what to do. That alone was enough to eliminate all of my panic when writing the blog, even when I wrote about my father directly, and gave me a sense of relief. I no longer dreaded it."

My friend and colleague Stephanie Smith is an educator, college and career readiness coach, and writer. Through her work with the Olga Lengyel Institute for Holocaust Studies and Human Rights, I know she values writing as a social justice tool and also as a tool for personal exploration. Recently we discussed the importance of writing prompts that might initially intimidate students. As an academic writer who writes largely about her own classroom research, she said she rarely had the opportunity to write about her personal life until she worked with the National Writing Project. I asked her why that writing was so powerful.

> I didn't feel the sense of fear and censure I might have felt otherwise because when I responded to those prompts, I was just talking to myself. Secondly, I was never afraid to share during those sessions because there was always a safety net of community. I think those kinds of prompts may be the only time students might be honest with themselves, so they are incredibly important prompts.

Prompts that may cause fear are not designed to out anyone, but offered as an invitation for self-exploration. The kind of healing self-talk that exists between students and their notebook can be some of the most cathartic and revelatory writing they do. Teachers may initially avoid these kinds of prompts to avoid overly solipsistic, navel-gazey prose. Novelist Zadie Smith (2018) says, "It's important to be that honest with yourself and it's important that you share that honesty with others, whatever their reaction is. Because sharing makes it bring forth fruit, and that's what makes it real. It has to have an audience to serve the larger purpose of creating and holding space for the other lives in the room." I feel these kinds of prompts—well crafted to produce highly personal writing yet insulated by an assurance of privacy—can benefit a student's ability to feel confident in other kinds of writing, such as argumentative and informative essays.

Fear of
Being a Fraud

I collect books about writing and writers. It's comforting to read professional writers describe how they revised a sentence two dozen times or
wrestled with an unruly paragraph for a month. Reading those experiences
puts me in their community of struggle in a way that feels instructive and
encouraging.

Eileen Simpson's (1982) *Poets in Their Youth*, for example, is a memoir about
her marriage to John Berryman, but also about writing and the lives of the poets
in their circle: Randall Jarrell, Elizabeth Hardwick, Delmore Schwartz, Robert
Lowell. Simpson traces the turbulence of their artistic greatness and mental
instability, the entirety of which could be summed up by lines from a Schwartz
poem: "Do they whisper behind my back? Do they speak / Of my clumsiness?
Do they laugh at me, / Mimicking my gestures, retailing my shame?" (25).

As the daughter of no-nonsense, farming stock, I confess some of their
torment strikes me as self-indulgent. But what is inescapable in Simpson's
memoir is the self-doubt the author and her cohort felt while writing. I feel this
as well. They were writing art, and I'm writing a resource book for teachers, yet
the self-doubt is the same: *Who am I to write a book? What new idea could I
explain that's not already obvious to everyone?*

Fear of being labeled a fraud hits a different spot than the fear of exposure
we discussed in Chapter 6. Less to do with emotional risk than with intellectual

inadequacy, it's the fear that whispers, *You have nothing to say; your thoughts are illogical, derivative, uncritical, trite.*

During the writing of this book, I have not been stumped by the technical aspect of writing (well, most of the time) nor have I worried about exposing something I would rather keep private, but I've often thought, *Am I the person who should be writing this book? What credentials do I have? Why should anyone listen to me?*

The fear of being unveiled as a hack leads to self-censoring, which shuts down the writing. In her second book, Brené Brown (2012) tells a story about writing her first book, *The Gifts of Imperfection.* She calls a friend for help, who asks, "What are your gremlins saying?" Brown defines *gremlins* as "messages of self-doubt and self-criticism that we carry around in our heads." Brown answers: "One's saying that my writing sucks and that no one cares about these topics. Another one's telling me that I'm going to get criticized and I'll deserve it. And the big one keeps saying, 'Real writers don't struggle like this. Real writers don't dangle their modifiers'" (78).

This feeling of not being good enough to express your thoughts or that your thoughts are lacking is felt across all fields of writing: imaginative, critical, and academic. Our students feel this deeply and often. Last year my writing classes watched the documentary *Born into Brothels* to analyze its rhetorical claim. When it came time to choose a subject for their own argument, Evelyn raised her hand to say what many students had on their mind: "Nothing has happened to me that's worth writing about. I wasn't born in a brothel."

"It's not the subject necessarily," I said. "It's the significance you bring to your subject."

"Who wants to watch a ninety-minute documentary about a kid growing up in Lexington, Kentucky?" said Marley.

Shayda then raised her hand. "Growing up has been done before. Like, a hundred times."

"Well, it hasn't been done before by *you*," I countered, unconvincingly.

What Is It?

Fear of being inadequate as a writer has its source in general feelings of shame. Psychologists call shame "the master emotion" because it demeans our sense of self-worth (Pincott 2019), where our imagination, ideas, values, and opinions all stem from. Writing is born there as well. If your gremlins whisper "not smart enough" and "not good enough," then writing, as a practice marked by failure and perpetual revision already, will be excruciating.

Although negative self-talk stems from this master emotion, how writers are taught in a classroom can be a contributing factor as well. Writing presented or perceived as an exercise in correctness instead of an exercise in discovery can cripple the writer and harm the work. In *Writing with Power*, Peter Elbow (1981) maintains writing requires both creation and criticism of equal measure, but at different moments: creation for the early moments of writing and criticism for the ruthlessness of editing. The problem I've witnessed with my students, however, is the conflation of these two postures. Students launch with creativity but are quickly slapped down by their critical voice. Shaping an idea, not even fully formed, in the presence of a hectoring voice, may lead to a complete block.

Unfortunately for many students, education is a twelve-year-long date with the critical voice. Although we urge students to speak their truth and honor their experiences, nearly everything about school runs counter to that. Most elementary school students are their own favorite writer, but as they rise in the system—a system that consistently urges them to replace their voice with something more formal, more academic—they lose their writerly self-regard.

When I started teaching at Morehead State University in the late '90s, I was told a story about a history professor from the Pacific Northwest who taught at Morehead for more than a decade. On the first day of class during his first year, he mispronounced a student's name. She did not correct his pronunciation that day or any day following. During finals week, he heard another student say her name and realized his mistake.

"Why didn't you tell me?" he asked.

"You're the professor," she said. "I figured you knew better than me."

I heard this story in 2002, and the professor had been gone for many years, so we could file it under "Mistakes We Don't Make Anymore," but the larger point of this story, for me, is the enduring notion that because teachers know more about their field of study, they also know more about everything in general. Even something as intimate and personal as one's own name. Or the style of one's own voice.

This notion that a teacher knows best can have disastrous consequences when it comes to helping students discover their writing style. And in a hundred tiny unspoken ways, students perceive that not only are their ideas underdeveloped, but they, as writers, are not up to the job either.

Without a doubt, the greatest casualty is student voice, which is the main artery of style in the writer. When SAT 500 words and academic-sounding phrases are substituted for a student's vocabulary and pattern of speech, the writer's voice is maligned and the sure footing of thought is disrupted. Students need practice finding and using their own voice. They also need to understand how voice and style choices need to be consistent and coherent within each writing task they take on. The voice and style for one task may not be appropriate for another. Knowing when to zig and zag rhetorically and using your voice to do it is part of developing writerly self-regard.

Prose needs an assured voice to deliver it. Timidity and insecurity in the writer lead to timidity and insecurity in the writing. If a student has been assigned a topic, assigned a position on that topic, assigned research to review for that topic, then given an organizational form in which to write, why would a student go to the trouble of trotting out an original thought in his original voice? These assignations are done mostly to save time in the classroom and to support learning for writers, which is not without merit. But lack of autonomy often leads to feelings of illegitimacy, which undercuts student growth far more than not knowing how to document a source in MLA style.

Many writers feel like a critical voice inside their head accuses them of being fake when they attempt to write. Maybe it's a teacher's voice or a peer who laughed at you when you shared a poem in class. Have you encountered this kind of voice? What does it say to you? How do you overcome it?

7-1

Although writing instruction has come a long way from essays drenched in red ink, students still associate writing assignments with correctness and editing marks like *frag* and *awk*. How do you balance protecting a student's own choice and voice with the need to reinforce good writing skills?

7-1

How Does It Manifest in Writers?

Poets in Their Youth (Simpson 1982) is a chronicle of self-destruction, infidelities, incarcerations, and hospitalizations. Berryman himself jumped to his death into the icy Mississippi River convinced his best work was behind him, and Schwartz died alone in the hall of a seedy Times Square hotel, lying there for two days before anyone found his body. And history is littered with writers who use addiction to medicate insecurity or mental illness.

Fortunately, most of us only suffer from the minor deadlocks when it comes to facing our own inadequacies. I encourage students to write about these fears before they write about anything else. To address the fear before it's fetishized as an aesthetic is important especially for my gifted writers, who may see literary suffering as a first step to success. I do this by sharing stories of my own process as well as my own self-doubts. Talking about this fear of inadequacy helps students probe its power, and the fear of fraud doesn't seem as special, as precious, or as scary.

As with the fear of exposure, writer's block, procrastination, and perfectionism are typical responses, but I also want to illuminate three specific reactions to the fear of fraud: feeling like an imposter, listening to negative self-talk, and limiting your writing by comparison.

Look back over your life as a student. What is one writing assignment or task where you felt you weren't up to snuff? How did you deal with the feelings of inadequacy or incompetence? How could you share your experience with another student going through the same thing?

A student's thoughts on a topic like gun control are central to her writing, but her thoughts alone, or an unexamined opinion, do not make an argument. How do you teach students that their opinions must be informed by research and evidence while still encouraging their own voice and centering their thoughts?

Feeling Like an Imposter

So named in 1978 by American psychologists Suzanne Imes and Pauline Rose Clance, the term *imposter syndrome* applies not only to writers, but entrepreneurs, actors, politicians, and just about anyone who takes a leap into uncomfortable creative territory (Stein 2016, 37). Although this syndrome can be found in almost any demographic, imposter syndrome seems to strike those who've been labeled as "gifted" the hardest. Imposter syndrome also plagues populations such as women, people of color, or people born in poverty who have had doors closed to them in the past and may have internalized feelings that their accomplishments are delivered from a source other than their hard work and talent.

Imposter syndrome, simply put, is the feeling you haven't earned your achievements. Through some stroke of luck or a mistake you've managed to be awarded success, and it's just a matter of time before everyone knows you're a fraud. My gifted students feel this sharply. "When I first came to this program and I was listening to everyone read their work on the first day, I was thinking, 'I'm in the wrong class. I'm not that good,'" said Kate in a roundtable discussion we had on the subject.

Despite success, writers who suffer from imposter syndrome tend to downplay their achievements. Kentuckian Kayla Whitaker (2017) has written about her yearlong battle with depression after the publication of her first book, *The Animators*. Whitaker grew up in a town where I once lived and ran a bookstore. Kayla was one of a group of kids who showed up at our monthly poetry readings and read her work. She had the goods. She was an incredible wordsmith who possessed both vision and rhythm.

Kayla left Kentucky, went to college, then was admitted to a great MFA program. "It was, I was convinced, absolutely stupid luck. I was thrown into classes with people who'd gone to amazing schools—Ivy League, private, rarified. I was absolutely numb with intimidation. 'They belong here,' I thought. I did not."

She eventually published a novel, which was well received and applauded, but she couldn't shake the feeling of her own inadequacy. "I thought getting a novel published would make me elated. Instead, it created crippling self-doubt."

Even gifted students, like Kayla, often feel like an imposter in school. School is an experience that other kids know how to do, but students with social anxiety feel like outsiders. If they ace a quiz or get a distinguished grade on their essay, they may internalize it as luck or chance or the teacher taking pity on them. Students who come from families who, due to religious, familial, or regional acculturation, have a high shame response to achievement are especially vulnerable. If their community perceives success at school as a display of pride or arrogance, students may not want to broadcast those accomplishments or may dismiss them to preserve their inclusion in the neighborhood. Whitaker writes of this with regard to being raised in the evangelical South: "I am secretly convinced a universal force will punish me, in one way or another, not only for aspiring to be something I am not but for feeling such paralyzing sadness at an event I know I am lucky to experience, one that might not happen again."

7-3

7-3

> Have you ever felt like a reader is going to "find you out" when they read your writing? Have you ever felt like a fraud when you write? What did that feel like? How did you overcome it to write? Write for five minutes, then share your experiences. Are the experiences similar or different? What patterns of commonality emerge?

Listening to Negative Self-Talk

"Where is this coming from?" I sat on the couch in our classroom with a student, her chest heaving with sobs.

"From this class!" she wailed.

She'd spent the last five minutes recounting how badly she had done on an assignment: a one-sentence logline that summed up a movie script she wanted to write.

With student permission, I had copied each of their loglines for a creative project on large sheets of butcher paper. The papers were taped on the walls, and the assignment had been for the class to gallery walk around the room and ask questions and make connections.

"I feel like I'm being called an idiot," she cried.

Previously, I had walked around the room as this assignment was going on. I saw no criticisms or callouts, only curious questions and "Hey, this reminds me of . . ." connections.

A fresh new wave of sobs racked her body. We talked for several minutes until my next class showed up. Although I didn't convince her of her classmates' support and goodwill, one thing was clear to me: the calls were coming from inside her own head.

Everyone has an inner voice. It's the one I heard this morning as I dawdled over my second cup of coffee when I had promised myself the night before I would take an early morning run. Inner voices can urge us to act kindly toward others, remind us to call our mother, or to drink ten glasses of water daily. They serve as gatekeepers to our egos and exist as a healthy function of a mature mental state. But when a student's inner voice becomes toxic and ever present—*Just who do you think you are? Everyone is laughing at you. Don't do it!*—the voice triggers destructive thought patterns and can shut down his writing. Students with social anxiety may experience distorted thinking, such as catastrophizing situations, such as my student did.

One of the surest sources of shame is the voice we alone hear, tuned by our personal history and our families of origin. Students who are raised in critical households, who are members of toxic friend groups, or who have been victims of a bullying teacher often store *that* voice in their head, which emerges anytime they attempt to do anything creative. These "shame tapes" (Brown 2012, 66) create an endless cassette of negative self-talk we've cultivated and nourished to somehow protect ourselves from rejection and ridicule.

All of us have voices inside our heads. Some of them encourage us to do our best, but others invite us to be self-destructive. Other voices shut down our creativity and personality. Make an inventory of the different voices you hear when you attempt to do something outside your comfort zone. Where did these voices originate? Whom do those voices belong to? Are some of them positive and encouraging? Are others negative and discouraging? After writing for five minutes, share your findings with your class. Discuss the patterns of commonality that emerge.

7-4

7-4

As children mature and begin to question and challenge their parents, their faith, their neighborhood, or their friend group, they might be accused of "getting too big for their britches" or "getting above their raising." In many rigid communities, blind acquiescence to the rules of the community is a virtue and to question is a vice. Have you experienced this in your own life? How did this threat of "Who do you think you are?" help or hinder your progress as a writer? Write for five minutes, then share your experiences. Are the experiences similar or different? What patterns of commonality emerge?

7-5

7-5

Comparing Yourself to Others

Kate was a student who came into our program as a freshman, and from the first day of class compared herself to others and bemoaned this fact to me during every conference.

"But everyone else's ideas are so much better than mine," she confided.

"Why do you say that?" I said.

"Because they are. When I hear Evelyn's ideas, mine sound so dumb."

"Writing isn't a competition."

She looked at me as if I were daft. "Of course it is! It's how people get into colleges and into good schools. I'm going to have to go to a state school."

As a proud graduate of three state schools, I bit my tongue and carried on.

Comparison and competition are common in all human activities. For students who are raised by competitive parents, the idea that school is a journey of intellectual self-discovery sounds ridiculous. Students who feel their academic efforts are constantly measured against an unobtainable phantom of excellence can feel anxious and defeated. They see writing as another measure of how inadequate they are.

In many ways, comparison can be a fire starter for creativity. Great historical swells of literature or art (Southern writers of the '30s, Italian artists of the Renaissance) may have been initiated by competition. Those expats living in Paris in the '50s were all trying to outdo each other with their work. Competition can be healthy; some students see it as a matchstick, but taken to the extreme, it can be destructive.

Students who see school as a competitive sport lose out on many of the joys of writing, such as self-discovery, in their effort to write The Best Essay Ever. Competition and comparison lead to self-doubt, toxic self-editing, and second-guessing, which can shut down writing in the first draft stage. Comparing your first draft to someone's final draft is an example of an unhealthy pattern of assessment. Comparing your voice or the fitness of your style is another debilitating habit writers fall into. Even comparing what you are writing in the present with what you envisioned producing can lead to shutdown.

7-6   Do you see writing as a competition? Does this heighten your desire to do the best that you could do or does it hinder your creativity by knowing that you have to "beat" other writers to "win"? Why do you think this way?

Here are five questions about comparison and competition. Choose one and write for five minutes:

7-7

- Do you feel competitive with your peers in social settings? How does that shape your social interactions?
- In what areas of your life do you compare yourself to others? Why?
- Are you raised by competitive parents? How has that shaped the way you see the future?
- Do you see school as a competitive environment? Why or why not?
- Is competition in school a healthy or unhealthy factor? Defend your answer with evidence from your life.

Look over your curriculum and analyze it through the lens of competition. What activities or assignments heighten the sense of competition between students in your classroom? Do these activities contribute to a safe and supportive classroom culture? Why or why not?

7-6

Students come to us with varied social and emotional histories. When you have students who grapple with shame or a negative self-image, how do you deal with that? At what point do you suggest students seek professional help to manage their social anxiety?

7-7

How to Use the Fear of Being a Fraud to Fuel Your Writing

All writers eventually make peace with their demons and use that energy to further their vision for writing. They may feel the fear, but they write through it, or despite it, or with the self-doubt at their back like a stout wind pushing them across the lake to their destination. The end product, while not as sparkling as the unwritten vision in their head, is out there for the world to see. And that's a pretty good return for vision. Reading about other writers' self-doubts reassures students this feeling is universal, but writing about their fears is also crucial to cultivating writing courage. How do we build similar courage in our students and ourselves? Here are six strategies to try out.

Build a Robust Skill Set

When writers don't have the skills, it doesn't matter what they write because they feel like it's all going to be "bad." Improving basic student writing—how to construct a logical sentence, how to arrange a paragraph as the power unit of an argument—will help students feel confident to express their inner truths. They may have the most insightful, brilliant point in the world, but without the technique to telepath that to the reader, their shame shuts them down before they can get started.

Students do learn to write by writing, but intentional craft lessons and direct instruction about how language and arrangement work are crucial. Mastering the mechanics of writing can only be achieved by the genuine labor of writing, trial and error. And more trial, and more error, and more trial. This process includes the writer knowing the basics of writing—a subject agreeing with a verb to make a sentence, for example—and it works outward from there. Confidence in their skill contributes to confidence in students' process: they feel sure they can be successful, even if their early drafts are shaky.

Writing is ultimately an exercise of creative problem solving; without those skills, students flounder to communicate their vision to an audience. Dancer and choreographer Twyla Tharp (2003) calls this a "failure of skill." "If you don't have a broad base of skills, you're limiting the number of problems you can solve when trouble hits" (222).

Ways to Help Students Build a Robust Skill Set

- Teach students grammar and usage using their own sentences and paragraphs as examples. When I confer with students, I like to pull out one or two sentences or a couple of paragraphs and demonstrate how to manipulate their own language to put emphasis on different parts of the sentence.

  » Teach students how to cut sentence fat and add sentence fat. Pull a sentence from their essay and ask them to expand and contract the sentence by cutting away fat, then adding fat to it, then cutting it away again.

  » Rewriting sentences in multiple ways is a great way to practice micro-revision. It helps students to break out of the notion there's only one right way to write a sentence.

   » Write several different transitions between two paragraphs to demonstrate the power of "trying on" transitions to confer logic and chronology between ideas. Show students how transitions create clearer connections between the ideas housed in two paragraphs and how to test them on for soundness.

- Introduce the concept of macro- and micro-revision, looking at the big picture and the tiny elements of prose while playing around with individual words and sentences.

   » Model your editing process for your students. Model the elimination of wordiness in your own writing. Show students how to identify wordy clutter in their paragraphs and excise it for clarity.

   » Explain how to switch up subordinate and main clauses to couch the power of the sentence in the main clause, for example.

   » Showcase examples of active and passive voice from their own writing as a demonstration of how to confer clarity and power to the content.

   » Explain how sentence combining can be powerful, but sometimes it is not.

   » Show students how professional writers use fragments, two-word sentences, or one-sentence paragraphs or start a sentence with a conjunction to create emphasis and logic.

- Assess student skills on the fly. During one-on-one conferences, ask kids to explain how their ideas are connected on a sentence level and on a paragraph level.

   » Figure out where the error in logic or tension or pacing is occurring, and help them see how to reframe the sentences or paragraphs for better flow.

   » Give students many, many, many opportunities to practice summarizing and paraphrasing in their own words. It's one of the skills I use most frequently in my writing life.

- Teach craft minilessons on global elements, like tension and structure and tone, using mentor texts where students can see the big picture of the text.

   » Ask them to read these texts forensically, looking for the bones and ligaments and tissues that hold the piece together.

   » Use mentor texts to show students how to vary sentence length for rhythm and power, how to use language to surprise the reader, how to use evidence to persuade, and so on.

   » Create a rich library of mentor texts and teach students how to find sentences and writing styles they like to try them out in their own writing.

(For additional resources on this point, check out *A Teacher's Guide to Mentor Texts* [Marchetti and O'Dell 2021].)

- Talk about language incessantly and passionately.

  » Talk about your favorite words, new words you've learned from reading or from your students.

  » Talk about the political and geographic history and connotative substructure of standard and nonstandard words.

  » Track the evolution of a trendy word from its first use to its present iteration. Introduce students to *Lexico*, *Oxford English Dictionary*, and *Urban Dictionary*.

  » Ask students to reflect on their favorite words, the words they use the most. Ask them to keep a vocabulary register, which tracks how many times a day they say a particular word or phrase.

  » Increase students' writing capacity by increasing their capacity to learn, store, and later use a rich vocabulary.

- Have students read their work out loud to a partner or small group. I know this is a big ask for middle or high school students, but it's one of the most powerful things we do. If you model reading your own work out loud, followed by vulnerable inquiry, you set the tone for future readings in a safe and supportive environment. Reading out loud creates such a communal bond between peers, and it allows the reader to hear where the writing stumbles, where a word has gone missing. When students want to have a revision conference with me, the first question I'm going to ask them is "Have you read this out loud yet?" If they haven't, they need to do that first, either alone or with a peer.

Become a Deep Researcher

In an undergrad writing class, I remember our professor railing about fiction writers who got things *wrong* about nature, like having peonies blooming in late summer when they actually bloom in spring. Lack of basic research signaled that the writer hadn't cared to check out the accuracy of the detail. As we discussed a peer's short story, I remember thinking: wow, writers need to know *everything*. To help students eradicate fears of fraud, teach them to be sticklers for nailing down research and checking facts. Here are a few ways to think about research as a means to build a student's confidence as a writer:

- Show students how to research widely and deeply. Teaching students how to cite and attribute quotes, how to access primary documents, and how to summarize secondary sources will all build a student's confidence as a writer.

- Teach students how to track and manage research. One of the biggest struggles I had in college was managing the sources I found, remembering where I had jotted down a fact, who said it, when it was said. Teach students how to keep a simple source list, how to bookmark articles, or how to create a reading list.

- Teach students how to fact-check themselves. Research widely to understand the scope of the topic under consideration, then settle into a claim based on the evidence. Find two or three compelling pieces of evidence for their claim, but then fact-check those details against multiple sources.

- Teach students how to fact-check each other. Every magazine employs someone who fact-checks articles and columns. This is standard procedure. Create a day where students follow the facts and check each other.

Doing your research is especially crucial if you plan on writing about someone who does not look like you. Writers approach this research with the awareness that they could do all the research but still get the voice wrong in the execution.

Foster Agency and Writerly Self-Regard

Students are more inclined to engage in writing when they are given choice about the topic. Agency plays a critical role in developing students' attitudes toward writing and their writing identity. Students who perceive they have little to say and less to say it with will often deliver essays marked by tepid research and underdeveloped claims. Conversely, students who see themselves as a legitimate writer with a legitimate claim to their own topic will write with a greater degree of efficacy. Agency combats imposter syndrome by developing a student's writerly self-regard, and once self-regard is cultivated, the fear of being an imposter decreases. Social worker Sherry Amatenstein says, "It's an inside job. Once you can stop being an imposter to yourself, you won't feel anymore that you're an imposter to the world" (Stein 2016, 39).

Fostering agency helps students develop their own writing style as well. They begin to trust their own process, topics, and organizational strategies. Even in a classroom where a district-mandated or departmentally adopted writing program must be used, teachers can honor students' individual perspectives and takes. Introducing projects where students become experts on anything from frog gigging to magic tricks to TikTok can have a powerful impact on a student's independence as a writer.

Teachers can create a classroom environment that helps students develop agency and writerly self-regard by allowing them to choose their own topics, map out their own research, and struggle productively with writing. Here are a few strategies:

- Cultivate a writing climate where students respect each other's stories and where developing agency is a primary classroom expectation.

- Teach students how to advocate for feedback from peers, like professional writers do, and frame their own success criteria based on their goals.

- Ask students to take control of their writing from inspiration to publication through the use of a project-based writing approach.

- Challenge students to track how they use their writing time for one week.

- Repeat the maxim that writers are the final arbiter of their own work.

- Encourage students to become authorities not just about their own writing topics, but on the craft of writing itself.

- Explain the concept of agency and writerly self-regard to students and ask them to discuss why respecting student voices and opinions is vital to a writing community.

- Think about how to revise assignments so that students shape the driving questions or the process or the product.

Cultivate Voice and Style

When I am writing about topics I understand or people I know, my voice has confidence, authority, even lightness. My style is sharper, sentences shorter, language leaner and more exact. When I notice I'm writing with inflated language and janky syntax, I've drifted into boggy territory. Usually this kind of writing is delivered in a voice that sounds academic and not Liz. When we are obsessed with a topic and we learn everything we can about it, we feel confident in writing about it. That confidence emerges as the voice emerges. I tell students: "When your voice sounds like someone you don't recognize, you've veered off the path of your own authority."

We develop our voice by first recognizing its authority to speak the truths we believe in, and we maintain it through inquiry. If a student's thoughts (and voice and style) are not held in esteem by the student, then how will he feel authentic enough as a writer to write arguments that appeal to and convince an audience? If everything a student attempts to write is deemed shallow, then there's not much of a leap for that student to think *she* is shallow and her voice unfit. Our job is to assist students in the improvement of writing skill, but writing, at its core, is an exercise in critical thinking, the engine of which is self.

Imagine Your Best Audience

In an interview with *60 Minutes*, correspondent Jon Wertheim (2020) asked young adult novelist John Green whom he envisions as he writes.

"I don't envision a reader," said Green.

"You don't," Wertheim said.

"I think in some ways I'm writing back to my high school self to try to communicate things to him, to try to offer him some kind of comfort or consolation."

Green taps into a fundamental notion about writing: that we write primarily for ourselves. We are our first and best audience.

The works of Michel de Montaigne, the father of the modern essay, appear to have been written without an audience outside Montaigne's own mind. When he retired to his country estate in 1571 at thirty-eight years old, he decided to entertain himself with writing in extreme frankness about anything, including sleep, sex, travel, death, books, bodily functions, birth, religion, politics, food, and so on (Kramer 2009). He writes, "I am myself the matter of my book."

Imagining an audience, even vaguely, helps a student shape and mold a piece of writing, but if the student imagines an audience of critics and hecklers and trolls, the experience will be unpleasant. Envisioning an audience who understands you is key.

When I am nervous about speaking to a group of people, I imagine my family, specifically my older sister, out there in the dark, cheering me on and championing my work. This rule can be translated to writing: always imagine your best reader is reading your work. Instead of focusing on an icy reception by a critical censor, picture someone who gets you, understands you, and wants to hear what you have to say.

Writing a college admissions essay, which has a lot of stakes riding on it, can be incredibly stressful. Caden, who had visited some colleges over the summer, learned that admissions officers weren't the intimidating people he had previously envisioned. "I had built up in my head an image of an old, pointy-nosed white guy who marks through essays with his red pen and proceeds to feed the whole application into a shredder."

His fear of writing college admissions essays diminished when he shifted his audience to the relatable, young readers he had met on college visits. "One described her evaluation process as sitting in a recliner, dog in her lap as she reads application after application in early January. This is the person I am going to be writing for."

Writing about the writing is an excellent way to flesh out the idea at the center of your essay; it also helps you envision a kind reader and it gives you the confidence to use your true voice. When students are faced with a high-stakes assignment, such as the Common App essay that may decide their future, ask them first to write a letter to someone who loves them *about* what they are going to write for the essay. Writing about the writing to an audience who gets and supports them will help them figure out what they want to say in a nonthreatening scenario.

Grow Self-Awareness, Lose Self-Consciousness

According to Pat Schneider (2003) in *Writing Alone and with Others*, the greatest threat to voice is self-consciousness. Our true voice emerges when we kick the editor out of our heads and just write. Self-consciousness listens to all the negative chatter in our head instead of listening to our inner self-worth and self-love.

I want my students to cultivate a balance that increases their self-awareness and decreases the self-consciousness that belittles them and keeps them small and unproductive. This balance, it seems, is born of humility and writerly self-regard. Possessing humility as a writer is a necessary posture to cultivate.

This humility is a partner of self-awareness, knowing who you are as a writer and what projects you can successfully complete, while also not letting the destructive inner chatter demoralize or defeat you. Colson Whitehead (2019) says it was fifteen years before he felt confident enough in his own writing ability to be able to tackle the artistic demands of the writing project that eventually became *The Underground Railroad*. Even though he had the idea much earlier in his life, he continued to pass on the project because he felt like he didn't have the talent to sufficiently do justice to the idea he had.

My most successful writing students are clear-eyed and aware of their writing foibles, but not debilitated by them. They look at their writing skill and seek to improve it, by practice and a steely-eyed assessment of their talent. They all share a maturity and a humility that allows them to see themselves as they are.

It's helpful to tell students that even writers who write mega best sellers one year are forgotten the next. Most of the creative work that we do will be forgotten in one generation, so it is important that the work we do is meaningful to us. Tharp (2003) has a ready answer for all the negative self-talk that crops up when she creates: "People will laugh at me? So what? Thirty-seven years later I'm still here. Someone has done it before? Honey, it's *all* been done before. I have nothing to say? An irrelevant fear. We all have something to say" (22). Tharp's confidence comes from having talked back, dismissed, and outlasted her gremlins. She's been creating all her life and knows self-doubt is part of the territory.

Moving students from self-conscious to self-confident is an ongoing work in the writing classroom. Using Figure 7–1 (front of handout), students can review a list of activities that they may or may not have tried, and using Figure 7–2 (back of handout), students can identify and create a replacement cassette for their negative self-talk to make that transformation take place.

Figure 7–1 ~ *Strategies to Crush Negative Self-Talk and Grow Self-Compassion*

In the following list, check off the approaches you have tried in the past to crush your negative self-talk and grow self-compassion. When you are finished, flip this handout over and brainstorm some positive affirmations.

☐ Become mindful of your inner chatter. Start listening for the negative language that bubbles up whenever you are faced with a writing task. Separating the critical voice in your head from the other more rational voices is the first step to ultimately shutting it down.

☐ Redirect negativity. Stopping your inner critic and leaning into more positive affirmations can be helpful. When your inner voice says, *You're no good at writing* or *You're never going to get this assignment finished*, replace that thought with a more positive, encouraging affirmation: *I'm going to get started now and give this assignment my best effort*.

☐ Check the language you use to talk to yourself. When you're dragging yourself severely, switch the degree of negativity by changing the internal dialogue from "I hate writing" to "I don't like writing right now." By moving from severe language to more objective and balanced, you move yourself closer to the reality of the situation instead of catastrophizing the task.

☐ Be kind to yourself. Talk to yourself as you would talk to a best friend or family member. Imagine how you would talk to a good friend who was having trouble getting started on a writing assignment and talk to yourself that way.

☐ Phone a friend. When you catch yourself going down a shame spiral with your inner critic, call a good friend and tell them what your inner critic is saying. Say out loud, "Listen to this malarkey that my head is telling me." Have a good laugh at your saboteur's expense.

☐ Set a timer. Dismantling your inner critic can be accomplished by measuring the time you're being held hostage. If you're wallowing in negativity about a writing task, give yourself a time limit. Tell yourself, *You can fret and fume about this for exactly five minutes.* When time is up, move on to more positive solutions.

☐ Put your inner critic on notice. Ask your inner critical voice what it's done for you lately. Talk back to it. Challenge its assertions—*You're a bad writer*—by countering with examples from the real world—*I struggle with writing just like Shakespeare and every writer throughout history*.

☐ Knock down the stakes. Sometimes we allow an assignment to grow in power until our entire self-worth depends on the writing being absolutely perfect. If you see your writing from the long view, it will cut your inner critic's firepower down by lessening the stakes. Ask yourself, *Will this writing assignment really matter in five years from now?* If not, don't sweat it. Most things don't matter all that much in the grand scheme of things.

Figure 7–2 ~ *Identify and Replace Negative Self-Talk*

In the left column, list all of the negative self-talk you hear inside your head when you begin to write. In the right column, write at least five positive, affirming statements you can use to replace the inner critical chatter.	
Typical Inner Critic Talk When I Write	**Positive, Encouraging Clapbacks**

Epilogue

Feel the Fear
and Write Anyway

My initial spark to write this book about writing courage was envisioned as a slim self-published volume of handouts I use with my students, but the more I pulled them together, the more I realized that writing courage isn't necessary for anyone who doesn't have a writing identity.

Hmm, that sounds like a book idea, I thought. *Wonder if Heinemann would be interested?*

They were.

Terror. Panic. *Good*, the voice of Donald Murray echoed in my ear. I was right where all writers find themselves.

I wrote the courage part first. Fast. It took me less than six months to type it up. It was practical, drawing on many of the activities and exercises I use every year with my students. Then came the part about writing identity.

I didn't know how to define *writing identity*, a term I had used loosely and recklessly for years. I knew there was a difference between being a writer and being an author. I knew writing, like reading and thinking, was a skill accessible to everyone, not just the gifted or the called. But what elements arrived at the page with a writer? What elements of her experience accompanied the writer when she stepped into a writing task? What about her memories, her language, her voice? How did that figure into identity?

I wrote a blundering chapter and sent it to Tom, my editor (*Bless him, Lord*), who kindly wrote back nice things about my writing, but then pushed me to drill down on all the squishiness.

He wrote, "That said, I had to wrestle with the chapter more than others, and this is not surprising since identity is such an elusive concept. I felt myself struggling to hold on to it as I read the chapter. In the opening paragraph you say that the writing identity is 'everything they bring with them when they pick up the pen.' But a concept that is everything is hard to write about." The rest of the email was equally illuminating. He asked what identities do for writers. What about authorship, mentors, favorite subjects, habits, and so on?

I knew what I needed: an operational definition of writing identity, a definition that was more than just an attitude or an authorial stance. It just so happened that this coincided with the pandemic shutdown of 2020. Whereas our normal teaching schedules would have made it impossible, suddenly I had access to teacher friends through Zoom. I met with colleagues and used them as test subjects and sounding boards; I tested new activities with my senior class, who was game for all kinds of rabbit hole discussions of self-identity, social identity, and their own writerly self-regard.

Finally I had a full draft, and I dropped it in the laps of my two trusted beta readers, Amanda and Chris. Three weeks later, I met with them excitedly, but it was clear I had made a classic structural mistake with the book. I had organized it in the order in which I had written it. I cannot tell you how many times I've said to students, "Just because it fell out of your head this way doesn't mean it's the most powerful arrangement for the reader." I heard my own words and got busy.

I went on a two-week writing retreat with my manuscript in tow. I flipped the contents of the last two chapters to become the first two chapters. I rewrote transitional paragraphs and moved them around five or ten times for good measure. I moved Chapter 2 into Chapter 4. I moved the previous Chapters 3, 4, and 5 to become what is now Chapters 5, 6 and 7, and I hacked another chapter to pieces, tucking its bits in here and there like rosettes on a wedding cake.

I came home, printed out the whole thing and started doing line edits, the kind of revision that makes a big-picture girl like me insane. In a further violent and aggressive attack on my sanity, the pump on my neighbor's pool started going bad, which made my tranquil back porch sound like the tarmac at LaGuardia. Mother Nature was stoking it up to nine billion degrees every day by noon, and some rando in the woods behind our house had decided to detonate all the fireworks in North America.

Finally I was finished with the edits and pretty satisfied with myself. Yet I realized I needed to write some sort of conclusion, some parting salvo, so I sat down with my "clips," the folder I throw all the trimmings from earlier chapters, and threw about two thousand words in a document, looking for a thread, a way to bring the two ideas of writing courage and writing identity together. I wrote one draft, then another, then another. At the end of last week, I had about seven drafts of an epilogue that was as wooden and dead as [please fill in your own simile here because (a) pool pump, (b) heat, (c) fireworks].

I had just about decided this was going to be an epilogue-less book. But last Sunday, I went to church (I asked for prayer for this epilogue, y'all) and my friend Kevin came up to me and wanted to hear about the book I was writing. As I described to him the gist of the book, I realized the very thing I'd been struggling with—the flawed organization, the muddy definition of terms, the daily misgivings and self-doubts, the negative self-talk—was what I was experiencing with the epilogue. It must have slowly been dawning on him too.

"Hmm," he said. "You could write about your own process, you know, the struggle to write? That would be pretty authentic, right?"

So here we are. The epilogue is written. I started this book not knowing exactly how the writing would work, but I performed the acts of writing until the writing emerged. I shut down the chatter. I overcame the fear. I acted like someone who is a writer.

In short, I wrote *in doubt* and figured it out.

Student MetaWrites

The following student MetaWrites are found throughout the book. You can use these MetaWrites for bellringers, class enders, or extended writing prompts for students' writing notebooks. If you want context for them, each MetaWrite is followed by a page number where you can find them in the book.

CHAPTER 4

When you sit down to write, how do you get started? Some writers outline their thoughts; some write without planning. Some writers draft in longhand but others compose digitally. What are some of the writing habits that help you in the writing process? Make a list of all the writing habits you've depended on in the past to help you write. (See page 78.)

Stephen King famously writes two thousand words a day; James Joyce, ninety (Ang 2020); Reynolds Price had a daily quota of twenty-seven lines on a legal pad because twenty-seven lines added up to one typed page (Murray 1990, 60). Why do you think a daily word count is a writing habit of so many famous writers? Do you write daily? Do you have a daily word count? How would meeting a daily word count help or hinder you as a writer? (See page 78.)

Where do you like to write? Outside in a park, on the Starbucks patio, on the benches outside the public library? Or do you like to write inside—in your bedroom? At the dining room table? Do you find that where you write influences what or how you write? Why or why not? (See page 81.)

4-4
Do you write on the weekends or in the summer? When is the best time for you to write? Late at night, after school, early in the morning? Do you find that when you write influences what or how you write? Why or why not? (See page 81.)

4-5
Writers continually develop skills throughout their writing life. What is one writing skill you feel very confident of? What is one writing skill you could teach to another student? Where did you learn this skill? How does this skill help you as a writer? (See page 82.)

4-6
Think back over the last two or three years of your life as a student writer. What is one writing skill you wish you could improve on? How could you learn this skill? From your teacher, a mentor text, a peer, a YouTube video, or a writing center? How would learning this skill benefit you as a writer? (See page 82.)

4-7
Think back over your reading life. Are there books that have formed your identity, books that are part of your "textual lineage"? In *The African-American Guide to Writing and Publishing Nonfiction*, Jewell Parker Rhodes writes a whole chapter on the importance of literary ancestors, the writers who are like your literary grandmothers and grandfathers. Who are your literary ancestors? What writers have you learned from and enjoyed? Why do you claim them as an ancestor? (See page 85.)

4-8
Think back over your writing life. What teachers come to mind as mentors of your writing skill? Can you think of a particular lesson that a teacher taught that improved your writing? What other mentors have you had as a writer? Have you mentored someone in writing yourself? (See page 85.)

4-9
David Sedaris said he found his voice by imitating other people, trying on the voices of Joan Didion and Raymond Carver, for example. "It's all part of discovering what you sound like. I think we all do that—we take a little bit of this, and a little bit of that, and we just kind of put it in a big kettle, and we find ourselves" (Strawser 2013, 46). What mentors have you found through reading? Are there writers you have imitated in style or voice? What mentor texts do you find yourself returning to over and over? Why? (See page 85.)

CHAPTER 5

Most writers feel anxiety or fear when they start to write. What does it feel like when you have blank page in front of you? Do you feel excitement or dread? Or a mix of both? What tricks have you used to get started on a writing assignment? (See page 95.)

5-1

Do you avoid writing tasks or do you jump right in and get started? If you avoid writing, how does the avoidance serve your writing goals? If you jump right in, how does this strategy serve your writing goals? (See page 95.)

5-2

Do you ever feel as though when you sit down to write you'll have nothing to say? That your mind will go blank? Have you ever had this feeling? What did it feel like? Why does starting a writing assignment create anxiety in writers? (See page 97.)

5-3

Have you experienced writer's block before? What did it feel like? What was the occasion of the block, and how did you resolve it? If you haven't experienced it, what do you do to get started writing? How would you help someone who is experiencing writer's block? (See page 99.)

5-4

Do you procrastinate writing assignments? If you do, are you more of an active procrastinator, doing something else like researching, or are you more of a passive procrastinator, avoiding the task of writing altogether? How does procrastination benefit or harm you? If you don't procrastinate, what are some of the strategies you use to get started with a writing task? (See page 101.)

5-5

In writer and blogger Tim Urban's 2006 TED talk "Inside the Mind of a Master Procrastinator," Urban introduces us to the three voices in every procrastinator's mind: The Rational Decision Maker, The Instant Gratification Monkey, and The Panic Monster. Using his own story of putting off his ninety-page senior thesis until three days before it was due, Urban explains how the mind of the procrastinator works. Watch this fifteen-minute talk at https://www.ted.com/talks/tim_urban_inside_the_mind_of_a_master_procrastinator. Do you identify with Urban's story? What are your big takeaways from this TED talk? (See page 101.)

5-6

5-7 Essayist Rebecca Solnit writes, "So many of us believe in perfection, which ruins everything else, because the perfect is not only the enemy of the good; it's also the enemy of the realistic, the possible, and the fun" (Gilbert 2015, 166). Do you agree or disagree with this statement? Do you or someone you know suffer from perfectionism? Has it ruined the real, the possible, and the fun you might have had with writing? Why or why not? (See page 102.)

5-8 Student writer Maggie writes about her expectations at the beginning of a writing project: "The hardest part of writing is being okay with what I've written. Right now, my vision is so clear but I'm already worried that what comes out on the page isn't going to be what I am picturing right now and it never is and I know it never will be. So I have to continue to struggle with myself and convince myself that what I've written is enough and good in itself." Have you ever felt the way Maggie feels? How do you keep going even when what you see on the page isn't what you wanted to see? How do you convince yourself that what you are writing is good enough? (See pages 102–103.)

CHAPTER 6

6-1 Does writing about your personal life make you feel uncomfortable or excited? Does argumentative or analytical writing feel "safer" than personal or expressive writing? Why or why not? (See page 119.)

6-2 Has the fear of embarrassment ever stopped you or stifled you from writing something? Were you able to overcome your embarrassment and continue writing or did you avoid the task altogether? What happened? (See page 119.)

6-3 How does it feel to share personal writing with other students in your class? Do you feel comfortable sharing your writing or do you feel your peers will judge you, instead of just offering feedback on your writing? Why or why not? (See page 121.)

6-4 In an interview with the *Paris Review*, Salman Rushdie (Gourevitch 2008) said, ". . . if you write about everywhere you can end up writing about nowhere. It's a problem that a writer writing about a single place does not have to face" (361). What does Rushdie mean when he says that writing about everywhere ends up as writing about nowhere? Where is the single place, either geograph-ically or emotionally, from which you write? Do you feel comfortable writing about your family, your community, your neighborhood? (See page 121.)

Do you prefer writing assignments that allow you to choose your own topic or do you like writing assignments that provide you with a topic? When faced with a choose-your-own-topic assignment, do you tend to choose a safe topic or one that challenges you? Why or why not? (See page 124.)

6-5

Have you ever chosen to write about a topic because you knew your teacher would like the subject? Did this feel like you were cheating yourself or was it necessary to just get through the class? Why do you think students choose to write about topics they know their teacher will like? (See page 125.)

6-6

Have you ever felt that a writing assignment was an intrusion into your personal life? How did you react? Could you have discussed this with your teacher and advocated for a different assignment? Why or why not? (See page 126.)

6-7

CHAPTER 7

Many writers feel like a critical voice inside their head accuses them of being fake when they attempt to write. Maybe it's a teacher's voice or a peer who laughed at you when you shared a poem in class. Have you encountered this kind of voice? What does it say to you? How do you overcome it? (See page 141.)

7-1

Look back over your life as a student. What is one writing assignment or task where you felt you weren't up to snuff? How did you deal with the feelings of inadequacy or incompetence? How could you share your experience with another student going through the same thing? (See page 142.)

7-2

The following three MetaWrites are designed to be written together in class, followed by a discuss to generate community between teachers and students. These MetaWrites are also listed in Appendix B: Teacher MetaWrites.

7-3

Have you ever felt like a reader is going to "find you out" when they read your writing? Have you ever felt like a fraud when you write? What did that feel like? How did you overcome it to write? Write for five minutes, then share your experiences. Are the experiences similar or different? What patterns of commonality emerge? (See page 144.)

7-4

All of us have voices inside our heads. Some of them encourage us to do our best, but others invite us to be self-destructive. Other voices shut down our creativity and personality. Make an inventory of the different voices you hear when you attempt to do something outside your comfort zone. Where did these voices originate? Whom do those voices belong to? Are some of them positive and encouraging? Are others negative and discouraging? After writing for five minutes, share your findings with your class. Discuss the patterns of commonality that emerge. (See page 145.)

7-5

As children mature and begin to question and challenge their parents, their faith, their neighborhood, or their friend group, they might be accused of "getting too big for their britches" or "getting above their raising." In many rigid communities, blind acquiescence to the rules of the community is a virtue and to question is a vice. Have you experienced this in your own life? How did this threat of "Who do you think you are?" help or hinder your progress as a writer? Write for five minutes, then share your experiences. Are the experiences similar or different? What patterns of commonality emerge? (See page 145.)

7-6

Do you see writing as a competition? Does this heighten your desire to do the best that you could do or does it hinder your creativity by knowing that you have to "beat" other writers to "win"? Why do you think this way? (See page 146.)

Here are five questions about comparison and competition. Choose one and write for five minutes:

- Do you feel competitive with your peers in social settings? How does that shape your social interactions?

- In what areas of your life do you compare yourself to others? Why?

- Are you raised by competitive parents? How has that shaped the way you see the future?

- Do you see school as a competitive environment? Why or why not?

- Is competition in school a healthy or unhealthy factor? Defend your answer with evidence from your life. (See page 147.)

Teacher MetaWrites

The following Teacher MetaWrites are found throughout the book. You can use these MetaWrites for personal writing prompts or use them to write together with your students. If you want context for them, each MetaWrite is followed by a page number where you can find them in the book.

CHAPTER 3

3-1 How do you feel about yourself as a writer? Where would you rank your writerly self-regard on a scale from 1 to 5, with 1 being "I am not a writer" to 5 being "I am a writer"? Why do you rank yourself this way? What experiences have formed this core belief about yourself? (See page 47.)

3-2 Who were your writing mentors? Teachers, writers, friends, writing community peers? What experiences shaped your life as a writer? (See page 47.)

3-3 How would you describe your writing process to your students? How would you characterize your writing skill? What strategies have you used to overcome writing resistance? What are your writing preferences? What are your writing habits? (See page 47.)

3-4 Select a writing assignment you often give your students during the course of the year. Perhaps it's a personal narrative, a sonnet, or an analytical essay. Imagine yourself as a student in your classroom. You've read the material, looked over the rubric, done the research. How do you proceed? Describe the process you would take if you were asked to write this piece of writing. Does it match with the process that most of your students take in writing? What is alike or different about your approach? (See page 47.)

Select a writing assignment you often give your students during the course of the year and write a model for your students. Save all the drafts, including any notes you take, research, zero drafts, feedback from peers, and so on. Find a space in your room where you can set up a minimuseum with all of these archives of your process for students to walk through and make observations about how you process writing. (See page 47.)

3-5

Think back over your formative writing life and tell the story of how you learned to write. What is an early memory of writing before you were in school? Did you observe your parents or older siblings writing? How did that impact your awareness of writing? Who taught you to write your name? Did you write letters before you entered school? Who taught you? Do you remember tracing letters? Did someone other than a teacher teach you to hold a pencil and write? What implements did you use to write? (See page 52.)

3-6

Think about the writing you did during your time in elementary school. What are one or two memories you have of writing in elementary school? Do you still have the writing? What were some of the writing assignments you remember from that time in your life? Were your experiences with writing mostly positive or mostly negative? (See page 52.)

3-7

Think about the writing you did during your middle and high school years. What are one or two memories you have of writing in middle or high school? Do you still have the writing? What were some of the writing assignments you remember from that time in your life? Were your experiences with writing mostly positive or mostly negative? (See page 52.)

3-8

Think about the writing you did during your undergraduate, graduate, or doctoral experience. What are one or two memories of writing during these years? Did you embrace or resist the rigors of academic discourse required in college classes? Did you take a class in creative writing, science writing,

3-9

nature writing, or another kind of writing, such as playwriting, poetry, or screenwriting? Did you ever visit the university writing center or receive tutoring in writing? Do you still have copies of your writing from this time in your life? (See page 52.)

3-10

Think about the writing you do on the job. What are one or two memories you have of writing an extended piece of writing (beyond short emails) that required planning and revision? Do you write models of essays for your students? Are you required to write a reflection as part of your personal growth plan? Do you regularly write with a group of peers? Do you regularly write and share with your students? What kind of professional writing have you done over the past five years? (See pages 52–53.)

3-11

In what way does your self-identity impact what you write about or the audiences for which you write? In what way does your socioeconomic status, race/ethnicity, gender, sexual orientation, and family of origin impact what you write about or the audiences for which you write? (See page 59.)

3-12

How has other people's perception of your socioeconomic status, race/ethnicity, gender, sexual orientation impacted what you write about? How you write? The audiences for which you write? The subjects you write about? (See page 59.)

3-13

How has being part of a specific social, political, or cultural community impacted what you write about? How you write? The audiences for which you write? The subjects you write about? (See page 59.)

3-14

Fiction writer Alice McDermott writes: "I write about Catholics because I am one, a cradle Catholic, and so I know the language and the detail. This saves me from having to do too much research. Because I am a Catholic, the language of ritual, its repetitions and refrains, appeals to me and so finds its way into my work" (170). What aspect of your identity is so instinctual and innate that you know "the language and the detail" of it? What part of your identity is so ingrained into who you are that you wouldn't have to research to write about it? How does the language and the detail of this identity find its way into your writing? (See page 59.)

CHAPTER 5

In Elizabeth Gilbert's (2015) *Big Magic*, she says fear and creativity are conjoined twins sharing the same womb, the same birthday, and a few vital organs. If you kill the fear, she contends, you also kill the creativity. "So I don't try to kill off my fear. I don't go to war against it. Instead, I make all that space for it. It seems to me that the less I fight my fear, the less it fights back. If I can relax, fear relaxes too" (25). Do you make space for your fear of the blank page? What techniques have you found for relaxing with fear instead of fighting against it? How could you model this technique for your students? (See page 95.)

5-1

In *Draft No. 4*, a collection of eight essays on the writing process, John McPhee (2017) says even after he became a *New Yorker* staff writer, he had misgivings about his abilities. "You would think that by then I would have developed some confidence in writing a new story, but I hadn't, and never would. To lack confidence at the outset seems rational to me. It doesn't matter that something you've done before worked out well. Your last piece is never going to write your next one for you" (19). How does a lack of confidence in your own writing seem like a reasonable response to a writing task? Do you agree or disagree that "it doesn't matter that something you've done before worked out well"? (See page 97.)

5-2

Contemporary novelist Jodi Picoult dismisses the idea of writer's block. "Think about it—when you were blocked in college and had to write a paper, didn't it always manage to fix itself the night before the paper was due? Writer's block is having too much time on your hands. If you have a limited amount of time to write, you just sit down and do it" (Charney 2017a). Do you agree or disagree that writer's block is just a matter of having too much time on your hands? What personal experience with writer's block informed your answer? (See page 99.)

5-3

Psychology Today poses five reasons why writer might experience writer's block: "you've lost your way; your passion has waned; your expectations are too high; you're burned out; and you're too distracted" (Reynolds 2015). I've experienced all of these, sometimes at the same time. Has any one of these blocked you before? Which one? How did you get beyond it? What strategies did you learn to model for students? (See page 99.)

5-4

5-5   Students need large blocks of dedicated class time to develop a writing idea, narrow their topic, outline or draft, and get feedback and revise. But that time can be unproductive if students are actively or passively procrastinating. Do you talk about ways to battle procrastination and self-sabotage? How do you balance the need for valuable unstructured writing time with its potential to trigger procrastination in some students? (See page 101.)

5-6   When you share your writing with your students, do you feel pressure for it to be perfect? In what way would showing your students imperfect drafts of your own writing lift the burden of their own struggles with perfectionism? In what way might sharing be a risk for you? (See page 103.)

5-7   Brown (2012) writes "Perfectionism is self-destructive simply because perfection doesn't exist. It's an unattainable goal" (39). Is there a conflict, in a student's perception, that a draft needs to be perfect to get a good grade? How can we help students to master a skill that depends almost entirely on them embracing the imperfection of creation? How can we demonstrate this paradox to our students? (See page 103.)

CHAPTER 6

6-1   Think back over your writing life—as an elementary school student, as a high school student, as an undergraduate or a graduate student. Can you remember a writing assignment in which you discovered something about yourself? What are some revelations you made about yourself through writing? (See page 119.)

6-2   Can you remember any writing assignment that asked you to step outside of your comfort zone? How did this assignment make you feel? Were you able to write despite those feelings? If so, how did you overcome the fear of exposure? If not, what happened? (See page 119.)

6-3   In "Dangerous Writing," an essay on the dangers and joys of exposure as a writer, novelist Tom Spanbauer writes, "As a child, raised Catholic, I was to be seen and not heard, and I was beaten any time I expressed myself. I was told never to show off. To never make a spectacle of myself. And here I am in front of you" (2016, 37). How can you, as a writing teacher, mitigate the embarrassment that students might feel while writing, while also encouraging students to take risks when choosing writing topics? How can you encourage the best work while helping the writer navigate potential ridicule and bullying? (See page 122.)

Examine two writing assignments you normally give your students. What fears of exposure might these assignments present to your students? What brainstorming or community-building exercises might benefit students who are fearful of an assignment that requires them to write about a deeply held belief or a valued tradition? How might you acknowledge or prepare them? (See page 122.)

6-4

Many writing assignments require little more than reading some research and writing up a summary of it. Yet even when teachers craft assignments that center a student's experience or that allow students to choose their own topics, a student could still "move away" from a challenging topic and choose a topic that is safe and easy. Consider the writing assignments you give in your classroom. Do you offer both self-selected and teacher-assigned topics? Which of these paths offers students more agency and autonomy? (See page 124.)

6-5

When students choose to write from an argumentative position that you disagree with, how do you mitigate your personal response and reach out to help them shore up their arguments? How do you assure students that your personal opinions will not mitigate your responsiveness as their teacher? (See page 125.)

6-6

Can you remember a student who has responded in anger to a particular writing assignment? What was the source of the anger? How could you have resolved it or attempted to resolve it? (See page 126.)

6-7

CHAPTER 7

Although writing instruction has come a long way from essays drenched in red ink, students still associate writing assignments with correctness and editing marks like *frag* and *awk*. How do you balance protecting a student's own choice and voice with the need to reinforce good writing skills? (See page 141.)

7-1

A student's thoughts on a topic like gun control are central to her writing, but her thoughts alone, or an unexamined opinion, do not make an argument. How do you teach students that their opinions must be informed by research and evidence while still encouraging their own voice and centering their thoughts? (See page 142.)

7-2

The following three MetaWrites are designed to be written together in class, followed by a discuss to generate community between teachers and students. These MetaWrites are also listed in Appendix A: Student MetaWrites.

7-3

Have you ever felt like a reader is going to "find you out" when they read your writing? Have you ever felt like a fraud when you write? What did that feel like? How did you overcome it to write? Write for five minutes, then share your experiences. Are the experiences similar or different? What patterns of commonality emerge? (See page 144.)

7-4

All of us have voices inside our heads. Some of them encourage us to do our best, but others invite us to be self-destructive. Other voices shut down our creativity and personality. Make an inventory of the different voices you hear when you attempt to do something outside your comfort zone. Where did these voices originate? Whom do those voices belong to? Are some of them positive and encouraging? Are others negative and discouraging? After writing for five minutes, share your findings with your class. Discuss the patterns of commonality that emerge. (See page 145.)

7-5

As children mature and begin to question and challenge their parents, their faith, their neighborhood, or their friend group, they might be accused of "getting too big for their britches" or "getting above their raising." In many rigid communities, blind acquiescence to the rules of the community is a virtue and to question is a vice. Have you experienced this in your own life? How did this threat of "Who do you think you are?" help or hinder your progress as a writer? Write for five minutes, then share your experiences. Are the experiences similar or different? What patterns of commonality emerge? (See page 145.)

7-6

Look over your curriculum and analyze it through the lens of competition. What activities or assignments heighten the sense of competition between students in your classroom? Do these activities contribute to a safe and supportive classroom culture? Why or why not? (See page 147.)

7-7

Students come to us with social and emotional histories that we are not professionally trained to diagnose or treat. When you have students who grapple with shame or a negative self-image, how do you deal with that? At what point do you suggest students seek professional help to manage their social anxiety? (See page 147.)

Appendix

Eleven Reproducible Handouts to Use with Students

Figure 2–1 ~ *What Makes Up Your Writing Identity?*

Your writing identity is made up of several things: who you identify as, the communities you identify with, and how you see yourself as a writer. When you sit down to write, you bring with you a combination of these identities. The chart below breaks down these elements to help you think about your writing identity.

Instructions: Describe your identities in the blank row below.

Self-Identity	Social Identity	Writerly Self-Regard
Describe how you see yourself: race/ethnicity, personality type, values, beliefs, attitudes, memories, gender, birth order, age, grade level or education.	*Describe the groups you are a part of: your culture, your community, your school, your socioeconomic class, your religious and political affiliation, your geographic place, plus clubs, organizations, associations, and so on that you align with.*	*Describe how you see yourself as a writer, including your writing influences, your good and bad experiences with writing, your memories of writing, writing habits, writing passion, and writing skills.*

Figure 3–4 ~ *How Does Self-Identity and Social Identity Influence My Writing?*

When you pick up a pen or open a Google Doc to write, your sense of both self-identity and social identity comes with you. How do these identities inform or influence what, how, and whom you write about?

Directions:

In the following cells, answer these questions:

- How does this element of your identity impact your writing?
- How does this element influence the topics you choose or the way you write?
- How does this element impact the audiences for which you write?

There are no right or wrong answers. You can write as much or as little as you would like. You can jot down bullet points or write in paragraph form.

Your Age	
Your Values	
Your Personality	
Your Grade Level	
Your Race or Ethnicity	
Your Nationality	
Your Gender	
Your Socioeconomic Status	
Your Religion or Belief System	

Figure 4–1 ~ *Inventory of Emotions Related to Writing*

Inventory of Emotions Related to Writing	
Think over memories you have of writing in school. What emotions or feelings often accompany these memories? Write down five emotions or feelings that surround memories you associate with writing for school.	*Think over memories you have of writing outside of school. What emotions or feelings often accompany these memories? Write down five emotions or feelings that surround memories you associate with writing outside of school.*

Figure 4–6 ~ *Student Self-Skill Assessment*

Name:_____

Describe the writing project you would like to do for this unit. Please include the form you want to write in (speech, blog, memoir, essay, short story, poem, etc.) and a short summary of your idea.

Circle all the skills you currently have that will help you with this project:

Brainstorming   Journaling   Freewriting   Mapping   Drafting   Listing   Clustering

Narrowing Your Topic   Picturing Your Audience   Researching   Outlining   Plotting

Storyboarding   Organizing   Interviewing   Taking Notes   Finding Sources

Evaluating Sources   Paraphrasing   Fact Checking   Documenting Sources

Writing Effective Sentences   Writing Effective Paragraphs   Choosing Effective Words

Reading Out Loud   Revising   Editing   Inquiring   Getting Feedback

Proofreading for Spelling and Grammar

Circle all the skills you would like to develop during this project.

Brainstorming   Journaling   Freewriting   Mapping   Drafting   Listing   Clustering

Narrowing Your Topic   Picturing Your Audience   Researching   Outlining   Plotting

Storyboarding   Organizing   Interviewing   Taking Notes   Finding Sources

Evaluating Sources   Paraphrasing   Fact Checking   Documenting Sources

Writing Effective Sentences   Writing Effective Paragraphs   Choosing Effective Words

Reading Out Loud   Revising   Editing   Inquiring   Getting Feedback

Proofreading for Spelling and Grammar

Describe your writing project.

Figure 4–7 ~ *Three Sentences × Thirty Days*

Objectives: Build writing fluency, generate writing ideas, practice looking at your life like a writer, practice summarizing, practice detail selection.

Instructions: Every day for thirty days, write two sentences to record one experience. Choose either a significant experience, like the arrival of a baby brother, or something insignificant, like watching some ducks swim in a pond. Allow the constraint of writing only two sentences to bring clarity and brevity to your observation.

Day 1	
Day 2	
Day 3	
Day 4	
Day 5	
Day 6	
Day 7	
Day 8	
Day 9	
Day 10	
Day 11	
Day 12	
Day 13	
Day 14	

(continues)

Figure 4–7 ~ *Three Sentences × Thirty Days* (continued)

Day 15	
Day 16	
Day 17	
Day 18	
Day 19	
Day 20	
Day 21	
Day 22	
Day 23	
Day 24	
Day 25	
Day 26	
Day 27	
Day 28	
Day 29	
Day 30	

Look back over your thirty days of three-sentence observations. What patterns emerge? What writing topics leap out at you? What experiences deserve exploring more in depth? Which of these experiences would you like to write about? Why?

Figure 5–1 ～ *What Is Blank Page Anxiety?*

All writers have experienced these three conditions at some point when faced with the blank page. Have you or anyone you know experienced these conditions? How did it feel? What was your experience? What story could you tell about how this anxiety felt? Jot down a description of what each feels like to you or an experience you've had with these states of mind.		
Writer's Block	**Procrastination**	**Perfectionism**

Figure 5–2 ~ *What Are Coping Strategies for Blank Page Anxiety?*

All writers have had to develop strategies to write with these fears. What are some of the strategies you or someone you know has tried in the past? What is an effective activity or intervention or technique that will help a writer overcome blank page anxiety? List three to five strategies to help someone struggling with getting started on a writing assignment.		
Writer's Block	Procrastination	Perfectionism

Figure 6–1 ～ *Analyze the Fear of Being Embarrassed as a Writer*

Below are three professional writers musing about writers who feel shame around writing or creating. Read the quotes carefully, and analyze what the writers are saying. In the space below, answer the following question: Do you agree or disagree with this statement? Why or why not?

"The moment that you feel that, just possibly, you're walking down the street naked, exposing too much of your heart and your mind and what exists on the inside, showing too much of yourself. That's the moment you may be starting to get it right." *Neil Gaiman said this during a 2012 commencement speech to graduates at the University of the Arts in Philadelphia who were pursuing jobs as artists in the world.*	*"Write what disturbs you, what you fear, what you have not been willing to speak about. Be willing to be split open."* *Natalie Goldberg (1986) wrote this in her book* Writing Down the Bones, *which helps people overcome their fear of writing failure.*	*"Any writing exposes writers to judgment about the quality of their work and their thought. The closer they get to painful personal truths, the more fear mounts—not just about what they might reveal but about what they might discover should they venture too deeply inside. To write well, however, that's exactly where we must venture."* *This is from* The Courage to Write, *a book Ralph Keyes (1995) wrote to help people overcome their fear of writing.*
Your Analysis:	**Your Analysis:**	**Your Analysis:**

Figure 6–3 ~ *Creating Boundaries Around Writing Topics*

In the first two circles, name the people who are in the communication level on the right as audiences and brainstorm and write down possible topics on the left with the corresponding circle.

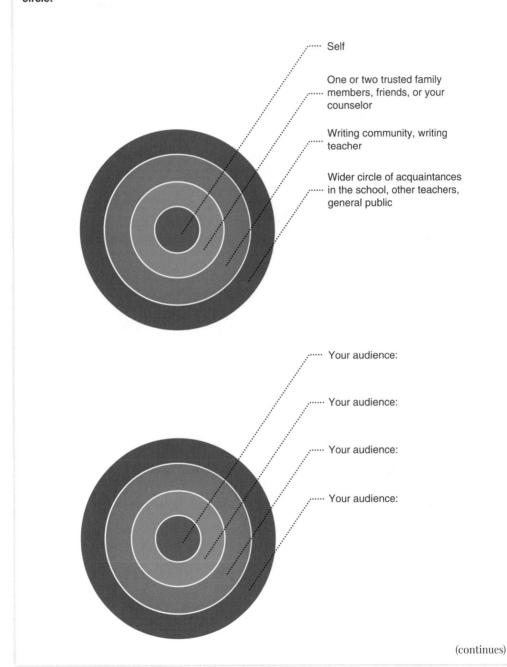

Self

One or two trusted family members, friends, or your counselor

Writing community, writing teacher

Wider circle of acquaintances in the school, other teachers, general public

Your audience:

Your audience:

Your audience:

Your audience:

(continues)

Figure 6–3 ∼ *Creating Boundaries Around Writing Topics* (continued)

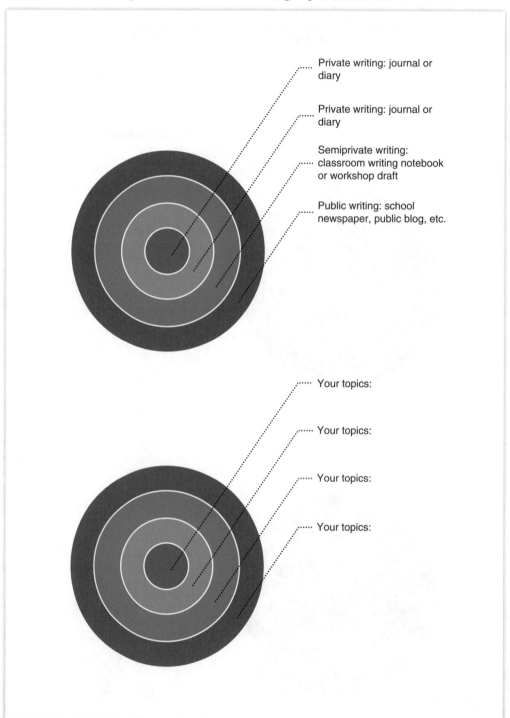

© 2022 by Liz Prather from *The Confidence to Write*. Portsmouth, NH: Heinemann. For more information about this Heinemann resource, visit: https://www.heinemann.com/products/e13280.aspx.

Figure 7–1 ~ *Strategies to Crush Negative Self-Talk and Grow Self-Compassion*

In the following list, check off the approaches you have tried in the past to crush your negative self-talk and grow self-compassion. When you are finished, flip this handout over and brainstorm some positive affirmations.

☐ Become mindful of your inner chatter. Start listening for the negative language that bubbles up whenever you are faced with a writing task. Separating the critical voice in your head from the other more rational voices is the first step to ultimately shutting it down.

☐ Redirect negativity. Stopping your inner critic and leaning into more positive affirmations can be helpful. When your inner voice says, *You're no good at writing* or *You're never going to get this assignment finished*, replace that thought with a more positive, encouraging affirmation: *I'm going to get started now and give this assignment my best effort*.

☐ Check the language you use to talk to yourself. When you're dragging yourself severely, switch the degree of negativity by changing the internal dialogue from "I hate writing" to "I don't like writing right now." By moving from severe language to more objective and balanced, you move yourself closer to the reality of the situation instead of catastrophizing the task.

☐ Be kind to yourself. Talk to yourself as you would talk to a best friend or family member. Imagine how you would talk to a good friend who was having trouble getting started on a writing assignment and talk to yourself that way.

☐ Phone a friend. When you catch yourself going down a shame spiral with your inner critic, call a good friend and tell them what your inner critic is saying. Say out loud, "Listen to this malarkey that my head is telling me." Have a good laugh at your saboteur's expense.

☐ Set a timer. Dismantling your inner critic can be accomplished by measuring the time you're being held hostage. If you're wallowing in negativity about a writing task, give yourself a time limit. Tell yourself, *You can fret and fume about this for exactly five minutes.* When time is up, move on to more positive solutions.

☐ Put your inner critic on notice. Ask your inner critical voice what it's done for you lately. Talk back to it. Challenge its assertions—*You're a bad writer*—by countering with examples from the real world—*I struggle with writing just like Shakespeare and every writer throughout history.*

☐ Knock down the stakes. Sometimes we allow an assignment to grow in power until our entire self-worth depends on the writing being absolutely perfect. If you see your writing from the long view, it will cut your inner critic's firepower down by lessening the stakes. Ask yourself, *Will this writing assignment really matter in five years from now?* If not, don't sweat it. Most things don't matter all that much in the grand scheme of things.

Figure 7–2 ~ *Identify and Replace Negative Self-Talk*

In the left column, list all of the negative self-talk you hear inside your head when you begin to write. In the right column, write at least five positive, affirming statements you can use to replace the inner critical chatter.	
Typical Inner Critic Talk When I Write	**Positive, Encouraging Clapbacks**

Appendix D

Suggested Reading List for Writing Courage

Bayles, David, and Ted Orland. 1993. *Art and Fear: Observations on the Perils (and Rewards) of Artmaking.* Santa Cruz, CA: The Image Continuum.

Brooks, Melanie. 2017. *Writing Hard Stories: Celebrated Memoirists Who Shaped Art from Trauma.* New York: Beacon Press.

Cameron, Julia. 1992. *The Artist's Way: A Spiritual Path to Higher Creativity.* New York: Penguin Putnam.

Caro, Robert. 2019. *Working: Researching, Interviewing, Writing.* New York: Alfred A. Knopf.

Chee, Alexander. 2018. *How to Write an Autobiographical Novel: Essays.* New York: Houghton Mifflin Harcourt.

Davis, Lydia. 2019. "Thirty Recommendations for Good Writing Habits." In *Essays One*, 226. New York: Farrar, Straus, and Giroux.

Dennis-Benn, Nicole. 2018. "Dear Beloved." In *Well-Read Black Girl: An Anthology*, edited by Glory Edim, 106–13. New York: Ballantine.

Faulkner, Grant. 2017. *Pep Talks for Writers: 52 Insights and Actions to Boost Your Creative Mojo.* San Francisco: Chronicle Books.

Gilbert, Elizabeth. 2015. *Big Magic: Creative Living Beyond Fear.* New York: Riverhead Books.

Goldberg, Natalie. 1986. *Writing Down the Bones: Freeing the Writer Within.* Boulder, CO: Shambala Publications.

Gourevitch, Philip, ed. 2006. The Paris Review Interviews. Vol. I. New York: Picador.

———. 2007. *The Paris Review Interviews.* Vol. II. New York: Picador.

———. 2008. *The Paris Review Interviews.* Vol. III. New York: Picador.

———. 2009. *The Paris Review Interviews.* Vol. IV. New York: Picador.

Johnson, Charles. 2017. *The Way of the Writer: Reflections on the Art and Craft of Storytelling.* New York: Scribner.

Johnson, Latrise, and Hannah Sullivan. 2020. "Revealing the Human and the Writer: The Promise of a Humanizing Writing Pedagogy for Black Students." *Research in the Teaching of English* 54 (4): 418–38.

Keyes, Ralph. 1995. *The Courage to Write.* New York: Henry Holt.

Lamott, Anne. 1994. *Bird by Bird: Some Instructions on Writing and Life.* New York: Anchor Books.

Legend, John, and Ta-Nehisi Coates. 2016. "John Legend and Ta-Nehisi Coates on the Art of Writing." *The Atlantic.* https://www.theatlantic.com/video/index/509651/john-legend-and-ta-nehisi-coates-on-writing/.

May, Rollo. 1975. *The Courage to Create.* New York: W.W. Norton.

McPhee, John. 2017. *Draft No. 4: On the Writing Process.* New York: Farrar, Straus and Giroux.

New York Times, The. Writers on Writing Complete Archive. https://archive.nytimes.com/www.nytimes.com/books/specials/writers.html?offset=-285.

Pennebaker, James W., and John Frank Evans. 2014. *Expressive Writing: Words That Heal.* Enumclaw, WA: Idyll Arbor.

Rhodes, Jewell Parker. 2001. *The African-American Guide to Writing and Publishing Nonfiction.* New York: Broadway Books.

Schneider, Patricia. 2003. *Writing Alone and with Others.* New York: Oxford University Press.

Toor, Rachel. 2017. *Write Your Way In: Crafting an Unforgettable College Admission Essay.* Chicago: University of Chicago Press.

References

Ang, Alvin. 2020. "Ten Legendary Writers and Their Daily Word Count." *The Writing Cooperative*, August 17. Accessed July 20, 2021. https://writingcooperativecom/10-legendary-writers-their-daily-word-counts-692c56cb97a5.

Arsten, Amy, Carolyn N. Mazure, and Rajita Sinha. 2021. "This Is Your Brain in Meltdown." Special Collector's Edition: The Science of Stress. *Scientific American* (Spring): 12–17.

Atwell, Nancie. 1998. *In the Middle: New Understandings About Writing, Reading, and Learning*. Portsmouth, NH: Heinemann.

Baker, Calvin. 2020. "The Best American Novelist Whose Name You May Not Know." *The Atlantic* (September). Accessed December 20, 2020. https://www.theatlantic.com/magazine/archive/2020/09/gayl-jones-novel-palmares/614218/.

Bayles, David, and Ted Orland. 1993. *Art and Fear: Observations on the Perils (and Rewards) of Artmaking*. Santa Cruz, CA: The Image Continuum.

Bettering American Poetry editors. 2016. "Voices of Bettering American Poetry 2015—Hanif Willis-Abdurraqib." VIDA Women in Literary Arts, August 22. Accessed April 25, 2021. https://www.vidaweb.org/voices-of-bettering-american-poetry-2015-hanif-willis-abdurraqib/.

Biss, Eula. 2007. "The Pain Scale." *Creative Nonfiction* 32 (1): 65–84. Accessed December 20, 2020. https://www.jstor.org/stable/44363570.

Bitzer, Lloyd. 1968. "The Rhetorical Situation." *Philosophy and Rhetoric* 1 (1): 1–14. http://www.arts.uwaterloo.ca/~raha/309CWeb/Bitzer(1968).pdf.

Boswell, James. 2014. *The Journal of a Tour to the Hebrides with Samuel Johnson, LL.D.* iBooks. Project Gutenburg. Posting Date October 9. EBook #6018.

Brooks, Geraldine. 2001. "Timeless Tact Helps Sustain a Literary Time Traveler." *The New York Times*, July 2. Accessed April 25, 2021. https://www.nytimes.com/2001/07/02/arts/writers-on-writing-timeless-tact-helps-sustain-a-literary-time-traveler.html.

Brooks, Melanie. 2017. *Writing Hard Stories: Celebrated Memoirists Who Shaped Art from Trauma*. New York: Beacon Press.

Brown, Brené. 2010. *The Gifts of Imperfection: Let Go of Who You Think You're Supposed to Be and Embrace Who You Are*. Center City, MN: Hazelden.

———. 2012. *Daring Greatly: How the Courage to be Vulnerable Transforms the Way We Live, Love, Parent, and Lead*. New York: Penguin Random House.

Butler, Octavia. 1995. "Furor Scribendi." In *Bloodchild: And Other Stories*, 137–41. New York: Four Walls Eight Windows.

Cameron, Jenny, Karen Nairn, and Jane Higgins. 2009. "Demystifying Academic Writing: Reflections on Emotions, Know-How and Academic Identity." *Journal of Geography in Higher Education* 33 (2): 269–84.

Cameron, Julia. 1992. *The Artist's Way: A Spiritual Path to Higher Creativity*. New York: Penguin Putnam.

Caro, Robert. 2019. *Working: Researching, Interviewing, Writing*. New York: Alfred A. Knopf.

Charney, Noah. 2017a. "Jodi Picoult on Writing, Publishing, and What She's Reading." *The Daily Beast*, July 13. Accessed December 2, 2020. https://www.thedailybeast.com/jodi-picoult-on-writing-publishing-and-what-shes-reading.

———. 2017b. "Maya Angelou: How I Write." *The Daily Beast,* July 11. Accessed December 2, 2020. https://www.thedailybeast.com/maya-angelou-how-i-write.

Chee, Alexander. 2018. *How to Write an Autobiographical Novel: Essays*. New York: Houghton Mifflin Harcourt.

———. 2019. "How to Unlearn Everything." *Vulture*, October 30. Accessed December 1, 2020. https://www.vulture.com/2019/10/author-alexander-chee-on-his-advice-to-writers.html.

Chodron, Pema. 1997. *When Things Fall Apart: Heart Advice for Difficult Times*. Boston: Shambala Publications.

Clear, James. 2018. *Atomic Habits: An Easy and Proven Way to Build Good Habits and Break Bad Ones*. New York: Avery.

———. 2019. "How Long Does It Actually Take to Form a New Habit? (Backed by Science)." James Clear. Accessed July 2, 2020. https://jamesclear.com/new-habit.

Critic at Large, A. 2004. "Blocked: Why Do Writers Stop Writing?" *The New Yorker*, June 14. Accessed January 1, 2021. https://www.newyorker.com/magazine/2004/06/14/blocked.

Daly, John, and Michael Miller. 1975. "The Empirical Development of an Instrument to Measure Writing Apprehension." *Research in the Teaching of English*: 242–49.

Davis, Lydia. 2019. "Thirty Recommendations for Good Writing Habits." In *Essays One*, 226. New York: Farrar, Straus, and Giroux.

Dennis-Benn, Nicole. 2018. "Dear Beloved." In *Well-Read Black Girl: An Anthology*, edited by Glory Edim, 106–13. New York: Ballantine.

DeSilver, Drew. 2019. "The Concerns and Challenges of Being a U.S. Teen: What the Data Show." Pew Research Center, February 26. Accessed April 25, 2019. https://www.pewresearch.org/fact-tank/2019/02/26/the-concerns-and-challenges-of-being-a-u-s-teen-what-the-data-show/.

Doidge, Norman. 2007. *The Brain That Changes Itself: Stories of Personal Triumph from the Frontiers of Brain Science*. New York: Penguin.

Duhigg, Charles. 2012. *The Power of Habit: Why We Do What We Do in Life and Business*. New York: Random House.

Elbow, Peter. 1981. *Writing with Power: Techniques for Mastering the Writing Process*. New York: Oxford University Press.

Eliot, T. S. 1963. *Collected Poems: 1909–1962*. New York: Harcourt, Brace and Company.

Faulkner, Grant. 2017. *Pep Talks for Writers: 52 Insights and Actions to Boost Your Creative Mojo*. San Francisco: Chronicle Books.

Fish, Stanley. 2011. *How to Write a Sentence and How to Read One*. New York: HarperCollins.

Flaherty, Alice W. 2004. *The Midnight Disease: The Drive to Write, Writer's Block, and the Creative Brain*. New York: Houghton Mifflin Company.

Forbes. 2021. "2021 American's Self-Made Women Net Worth: #80 Danielle Steel." August 24. Accessed December 1, 2021. https://www.forbes.com/profile/danielle-steel/#6159ba959edd.

Gaiman, Neil. 2012. Commencement address. University of The Arts, Philadelphia, PA. May 12. Accessed April 25, 2020. https://www.uarts.edu/neil-gaiman-keynote-address-2012.

Garner, Dwight, and Parul Sehgal. 2021. "19 Lines That Turn Anguish into Art." Close Read. *The New York Times*, June 18. Accessed June 21, 2021. https://www.nytimes.com/interactive/2021/06/18/books/elizabeth-bishop-one-art-poem.html.

Gilbert, Elizabeth. 2015. *Big Magic: Creative Living Beyond Fear*. New York: Riverhead Books.

Gipe, Robert. 2019. "The Mountains Aren't Enough: Understanding the Beauty, Complexity, and Universality of Appalachian Literature." Paper presented at NCTE Conference, Baltimore, MD. November 21–24.

Goldberg, Natalie. 1986. *Writing Down the Bones: Freeing the Writer Within*. Boulder, CO: Shambala Publications.

Gonchar, Michael. 2016. "650 Prompts for Narrative and Personal Writing." *The New York Times* Learning Network, October 20. Accessed June 12, 2018. https://www.nytimes.com/2016/10/20/learning/lesson-plans/650-prompts-for-narrative-and-personal-writing.html?module=inline.

Gonzalez, Rigoberto. 2016. "First." *Poets and Writers* (March/April): 89–93.

Gourevitch, Philip, ed. 2006. "Joan Didion: The Art of Nonfiction." In *The Paris Review Interviews*, vol. I, 473–500. New York: Picador.

———. 2007. "Toni Morrison: The Art of Fiction." In *The Paris Review Interviews*, vol. II, 355–94. New York: Picador.

———. 2008. "Salman Rushdie: The Art of Fiction." In *The Paris Review Interviews*, vol. III, 358–96. New York: Picador.

———. 2009a. "E. B. White: The Art of the Essay." In *The Paris Review Interviews*, vol. IV, 128–51. New York: Picador.

———. 2009b. "Haruki Murakami: The Art of Fiction." In *The Paris Review Interviews*, vol. IV, 335–70. New York: Picador.

Heard, Georgia. 2016. *Heart Maps: Helping Students Create and Craft Authentic Writing.* Portsmouth, NH: Heinemann.

Hemingway, Ernest. 1958. "The Art of Fiction No. 21." Interview by George Plimpton. The Paris Review 18. https://www.theparisreview.org/interviews/4825/the-art-of-fiction-no -21-ernest-hemingway.

———. 2012. *A Farewell to Arms: The Hemingway Library Edition.* New York: Scribner.

House, Silas. 2020. "Wendell Berry: The Poet of Place." *Garden and Gun* (April/May). Accessed June 2021. https://gardenandgun.com/feature/wendell-berry-the-poet-of-place/.

Iglesias, Karl. 2001. *The 101 Habits of Highly Successful Screenwriters: Insider's Secrets from Hollywood's Top Writers.* Avon, MA: Adams Media.

Jabr, Ferris. 2020. "Give Me a Break." Special Collector's Edition: The Science of Stress. *Scientific American* (Spring): 80–85.

James, Marlon. 2015. "From Jamaica to Minnesota to Myself." *The New York Times Magazine,* March 10. Accessed June 23, 2019. https://www.nytimes.com/2015/03/15 /magazine/from-jamaica-to-minnesota-to-myself.html?src=longreads.

Johnson, Charles. 1990. *The Middle Passage.* New York: Scribner.

———. 2017. *The Way of the Writer: Reflections on the Art and Craft of Storytelling.* New York: Scribner.

Johnson, Crockett. 1955. *Harold and the Purple Crayon.* New York: Harper Collins.

Johnson, Latrise, and Hannah Sullivan. 2020. "Revealing the Human and the Writer: The Promise of a Humanizing Writing Pedagogy for Black Students." *Research in the Teaching of English* 54 (4): 418–38.

Jones, Edward P. 2003. *The Known World.* New York: Amistad.

Kear, Dennis, Gerry A. Coffman, Michael C. McKenna, and Anthony L. Ambrosia. 2000. "Measuring Attitude Toward Writing: A New Tool for Teachers." *The Reading Teacher* 54 (1): 10–23.

Keyes, Ralph. 1995. *The Courage to Write.* New York: Henry Holt.

Koch, Stephen. 2003. *The Modern Library Writer's Workshop: A Guide to the Craft of Fiction.* New York: The Modern Library.

Konnikova, Marie. 2016. "How to Beat Writer's Block." *The New Yorker*, March 11. Accessed July 23, 2020. https://www.newyorker.com/science/maria-konnikova /how-to-beat-writers-block.

Kramer, Jane. 2009. "Me, Myself, and I: What Made Michel de Montaigne the First Modern Man?" *The New Yorker*, August 31. Accessed November 10, 2020. https://www .newyorker.com/magazine/2009/09/07/me-myself-and-i.

Kross, Ethan. 2021. *Chatter: The Voice in Our Head, Why It Matters and How to Harness It.* New York: Crown.

Lahiri, Jhumpa. 2011. "Trading Stories: Notes from an Apprenticeship." *The New Yorker,* June 6. Accessed November 14, 2021. https://www.newyorker.com/magazine/2011/06/13 /trading-stories.

Lamott, Anne. 1994. *Bird by Bird: Some Instructions on Writing and Life*. New York: Anchor Books.

Leader, Zachary. 1991. *Writer's Block*. Baltimore: The Johns Hopkins University Press.

Legend, John, and Ta-Nehisi Coates. 2016. "John Legend and Ta-Nehisi Coates on the Art of Writing." *The Atlantic*. https://www.theatlantic.com/video/index/509651/john-legend-and-ta-nehisi-coates-on-writing/.

Lieberman, Matthew, Naomi I. Eisenberger, Molly J. Crockett, Sabrina M. Tom, Jennifer H. Pfeifer, and Baldwin M. Way. 2007. "Putting Feelings into Words: Affect Labeling Disrupts Amygdala Activity in Response to Affective Stimuli." *Psychology Science* 18 (5): 421–28.

Louth, Richard. 2002. "The New Orleans Writing Marathon." *The Quarterly* 24 (1). Accessed July 20, 2021. https://archive.nwp.org/cs/public/print/resource/315.

Marchetti, Allison, and Rebekah O'Dell. 2021. *A Teacher's Guide to Mentor Texts, Grades 6–12*. Portsmouth, NH: Heinemann.

May, Rollo. 1975. *The Courage to Create*. New York: W.W. Norton.

McArdle, Megan. 2014. "Why Writers Are the Worst Procrastinators." *The Atlantic*, February 12. Accessed October 1, 2020. https://www.theatlantic.com/business/archive/2014/02/why-writers-are-the-worst-procrastinators/283773/.

McDermott, Alice. 2021. *What About the Baby? Some Thoughts on the Art of Fiction*. New York: Farrar, Straus and Giroux.

McPhee, John. 2017. *Draft No. 4: On the Writing Process*. New York: Farrar, Straus and Giroux.

Milkman, Katherine, Julia A. Minson, and Kevin G. Volpp. 2014. "Holding the Hunger Games Hostage at the Gym: An Evaluation of Temptation Bundling." *Management Science* 60 (2): 283–99. https://doi.org/10.1287/mnsc.2013.1784.

Minshull, Duncan. 2019. *Beneath My Feet: Writers on Walking*. London: Notting Hill Edition.

Mishan, Ligaya. 2019. "How Can I Silence My Fear of Failure When Starting to Write?" *The New York Times Style Magazine*, October 23. Accessed November 1, 2020. https://www.nytimes.com/2019/10/23/t-magazine/writing-fear-of-failure.html.

Morrison, Toni. 2004. *Beloved*. New York: First Vintage International Edition.

Mosley, Walter. 2019. *Elements of Fiction*. New York: Grove Press.

National Commission on Excellence in Education. 1983. *A Nation at Risk: The Imperative for Educational Reform*. Accessed November 6, 2021. https://edreform.com/wp-content/uploads/2013/02/A_Nation_At_Risk_1983.pdf.

New York Times, The. Writers on Writing Complete Archive. https://archive.nytimes.com/www.nytimes.com/books/specials/writers.html?offset=-285.

Newkirk, Thomas. 2017. *Embarrassment: And the Emotional Underlife of Learning*. Portsmouth, NH: Heinemann.

O'Dell, Rebekah. 2021. "Language Exploration That Changes Writers in 30 Minutes Per Week." *Moving Writers*, March 9. Accessed June 30, 2021. https://movingwriters.org/2021/03/09/language-exploration-that-changes-writers-in-30-minutes-per-week/.

O'Donnell-Allen, Cindy. 2012. "The Best Writing Teachers Are Writers Themselves." *The Atlantic,* September 26. https://www.theatlantic.com/national/archive/2012/09/the-best-writing-teachers-are-writers-themselves/262858/.

O'Shaughnessy, Kathleen, Connie McDonald, Harriet Maher, and Ann Dobie. 2002. "Who, What, When, and Where of Writing Rituals." *The Quarterly* 24 (4). Accessed July 20, 2020. https://archive.nwp.org/cs/public/print/resource/456.

Park, Jiyoung, Özlem Ayduk, and Ethan Kross. 2015. "Stepping Back to Move Forward: Expressive Writing Promotes Self-Distancing." *Emotion,* October 12. http://selfcontrol.psych.lsa.umich.edu/wp-content/uploads/2015/10/ContentServer.asp_.pdf.

Partnoy, Frank. 2012. *Wait: The Art and Science of Delay.* New York: Public Affairs.

Pennebaker, James. 2004. *Writing to Heal: A Guided Journal for Recovering from Trauma and Emotional Upheaval.* Oakland, CA: New Harbinger Publications.

Pennebaker, James W., and John Frank Evans. 2014. *Expressive Writing: Words That Heal.* Enumclaw, WA: Idyll Arbor.

Pincott, Jean. 2019. "Silencing Your Inner Critic." *Psychology Today,* March 4. https://www.psychologytoday.com/us/articles/201903/silencing-your-inner-critic.

Podsen, India, Charles Allen, Glenn Pethel, John Walde. 2013. *Written Expression: The Principal's Survival Guide.* New York: Routledge.

Prather, Liz. 2017. *Project-Based Writing: Teaching Writers to Manage Time and Clarify Purpose.* Portsmouth, NH: Heinemann.

———. 2018. "The Voice of the Wildcats." *Kentucky Living,* September 27. Accessed November 6, 2021. https://www.kentuckyliving.com/news/sports/the-voice-of-the-wildcats.

Proulx, Annie. 1999. "Inspiration? Head Down the Back Road, and Stop for the Yard Sales." Writers on Writing. *The New York Times.* May 10. https://archive.nytimes.com/www.nytimes.com/librarybooks/051099proulx-writing.html.

Rafanello, Donna. 2008. "Writing Well: It's All About Attitude." *Exchange* 181: 58–59. Accessed December 12, 2020. http://www2.csudh.edu/ccauthen/575S12/attitude-surv.pdf.

Reynolds, Susan. 2015. "Five Reasons You're Experiencing Writer's Block." *Psychology Today,* October 28. https://www.psychologytoday.com/us/blog/prime-your-gray-cells/201510five-reasons-youre-experiencing-writer-s-block.

Rhodes, Jewell Parker. 2001. *The African-American Guide to Writing and Publishing Nonfiction.* New York: Broadway Books.

Salesses, Matthew. 2021. *Craft in the Real World: Rethinking Fiction Writing and Workshopping.* New York: Catapult.

Saltz, Laura. 1998. "Revising the Draft." Harvard College Writing Program, Writing Center. Accessed May 2, 2020. https://writingcenter.fas.harvard.edu/pages/revising-draft.

Schneider, Patricia. 2003. *Writing Alone and with Others.* New York: Oxford University Press.

Schulten, Katherine. 2021. "100-Plus Mentor Texts for Documenting Your Life in 2020." *The New York Times,* March 13. Accessed April 25, 2021. https://www.nytimes.com/2020/10/15/learning/100-plus-mentor-texts-for-documenting-your-life-in-2020.html.

Scott, Elizabeth. 2020. "The Toxic Effects of Negative Self-Talk." *Verywell Mind*. February 25. Assessed July 4, 2021. https://www.verywellmind.com/negative-self-talk-and-how-it-affects-us-4161304.

Siegel, Ronald D. 2010. *The Mindfulness Solution: Everyday Practices for Everyday Problems*. New York: Guilford.

Simpson, Eileen. 1982. *Poets in Their Youth: A Memoir*. New York: Farrar, Straus and Giroux.

Spanbauer, Tom. 2016. "Dangerous Writing." *Poets and Writers* (January/February): 37–43.

Spera, Stephanie, Eric D. Buhrfeind, and James Pennebaker. 1994. "Expressive Writing and Coping with Job Loss." *Academy of Management Journal* 37 (3): 722–33. Accessed June 5, 2020. https://doi.org/10.5465/256708.

Stein, Leigh. 2016. "Poet, Writer, Imposter." *Poets and Writers* (May/June): 37–39.

Strawser, Jessica. 2013. "The Writer's Digest Interview: David Sedaris." *Writer's Digest* 93 (7). 42–47.

Tate, Claudia. 1985. "Toni Cade Bambara." *Black Women Writers at Work*. New York: Continuum International Publishing Group.

Tatum, Alfred. 2009. *Reading for Their Life: (Re)Building the Textual Lineages of African American Adolescent Males*. Portsmouth, NH: Heinemann.

Teicher, Craig Morgan. 2017. "Writing Badly." *Poets and Writers* (January/February): 39.

Temple, Emily. 2017. "Meet National Book Award Finalist Danez Smith." *Literary Hub*, November 7. Accessed November 1, 2020. https://lithub.com/meet-national-book-award-finalist-danez-smith/.

Terkel, Studs. 1989. "An Interview with James Baldwin." In *Conversations with James Baldwin*, edited by Fred L. Standley and Louis H. Pratt, 3–23. Jackson, MS: University of Mississippi Press.

Tharp, Twyla, with Mark Reiter. 2003. *The Creative Habit: Learn It and Use It for Life*. New York: Simon and Schuster.

Thomas, Lewis. 1995. *The Youngest Science: Notes of a Medicine Watcher*. New York: Penguin Books.

Toor, Rachel. 2017. *Write Your Way In: Crafting an Unforgettable College Admission Essay*. Chicago: University of Chicago Press.

Trex, Ethan. 2009. "Five Things You Didn't Know About Dalton Trumbo." *Mental Floss*, October 16. https://www.mentalfloss.com/article/23026/5-things-you-didnt-know-about-dalton-trumbo.

Urban, Tim. 2016. "Inside the Mind of a Master Procrastinator." TED talk. https://www.ted.com/talks/tim_urban_inside_the_mind_of_a_master_procrastinator.

Wapner, Jessica. 2020. "Secrets to Surviving Stress." Special Collector's Edition: The Science of Stress. *Scientific American* (Spring): 58–61.

Wertheim, Jon. 2020. "Author John Green: Reaching Young Adults and Dealing with Mental Illness." *60 Minutes*. CBS News, February 2. Accessed December 1, 2020. https://www.cbsnews.com/news/the-fault-in-our-stars-author-john-green-reaching-young-adults-and-dealing-with-mental-illness-60-minutes-2020-02-02/.

Wheeler, Lisa. 2004. "Writing About Place: The Writing WalkAbout." Paper presented at KCTE Fall Conference, Morehead State University, Morehead, KY. October 5–6.

Whitaker, Kayla. 2017. "My Imposter Year." *The Lenny Letter*, September 26. Accessed December 20, 2020. https://www.lennyletter.com/story/my-impostor-year-kayla-rae -whitaker.

White, E. B. 1969. "Notes and Comments." *The New Yorker*, July 19. Accessed May 1, 2020. https://www.newyorker.com/magazine/1969/07/26/comment-5238.

Whitehead, Colson. 2019. "I Have Been on a Fried Chicken Journey: 2019 AWP Annual Conference and Bookfair Keynote Address." *The Writer's Chronicle* 52 (2): 19–26.

Wilkinson, Crystal. 2014. Classroom presentation. Lafayette High School, Lexington, KY.

Wolynn, Mark. 2016. *It Didn't Start with You*. New York: Penguin Books.

Wood, Joanne V., W. Q. Elaine Perunovic, and John W. Lee. 2009. "Positive Self-Statements: Power for Some, Peril for Others." *Psychological Science* 20 (7): 860–66.

Zimmer, Carl. 2014. "This Is Your Brain on Writing." *The New York Times*, June 20. Accessed November 1, 2020. https://www.nytimes.com/2014/06/19/science/researching -the-brain-of-writers.html.